On the Private and Public Virtues of an Honorable Entrepreneur

Capitalist Thought
Studies in Philosophy, Politics, and Economics

Series Editor: Edward W. Younkins, Wheeling Jesuit University

Mission Statement

This book series is devoted to studying the foundations of capitalism from a number of academic disciplines including, but not limited to, philosophy, political science, economics, law, literature, and history. Recognizing the expansion of the boundaries of economics, this series particularly welcomes proposals for monographs and edited collections that focus on topics from transdisciplinary, interdisciplinary, and multidisciplinary perspectives. Lexington Books will consider a wide range of conceptual, empirical, and methodological submissions, Works in this series will tend to synthesize and integrate knowledge and to build bridges within and between disciplines. They will be of vital concern to academicians, business people, and others in the debate about the proper role of capitalism, business, and business people in economic society.

Advisory Board

Books in Series

On the Private and Public Virtues of an Honorable Entrepreneur: Preventing a Separation of the Honorable and the Useful, by Felix R. Livingston

The Ontology and Function of Money: The Philosophical Fundamentals of Monetary Institutions, by Leonidas Zelmanovitz

Andrew Carnegie: An Economic Biography, by Samuel Bostaph

Water Capitalism: Privatize Oceans, Rivers, Lakes, and Aquifers Too, by Walter E. Block and Peter Lothian Nelson

Capitalism and Commerce in Imaginative Literature: Perspectives on Business from Novels and Plays, edited by Edward W. Younkins

Pride and Profit: The Intersection of Jane Austen and Adam Smith, by Cecil E. Bohanon and Michelle Albert Vachris

The Seen, the Unseen, and the Unrealized: How Regulations Affect Our Everyday Lives, by Per L. Bylund

On the Private and Public Virtues of an Honorable Entrepreneur

Preventing a Separation of the Honorable and the Useful

Felix R. Livingston

LEXINGTON BOOKS
Lanham • Boulder • New York • London

Published by Lexington Books
An imprint of The Rowman & Littlefield Publishing Group, Inc.
4501 Forbes Boulevard, Suite 200, Lanham, Maryland 20706
www.rowman.com

Unit A, Whitacre Mews, 26-34 Stannary Street, London SE11 4AB

British Library Cataloguing in Publication Information Available

Library of Congress Cataloging-in-Publication Data

Names: Livingston, Felix R., author.
Title: On the private and public virtues of an honorable entrepreneur :
   preventing a separation of the honorable and the useful / Felix R.
   Livingston.
Description: Lanham : Lexington Books, [2018] | Series: Capitalist thought:
   studies in philosophy, politics, and economics | Includes bibliographical
   references and index.
Identifiers: LCCN 2018022608 (print) | LCCN 2018025541 (ebook) | ISBN
   9781498575584 (Electronic) | ISBN 9781498575577 (cloth : alk. paper)
Subjects: LCSH: Capitalism--Philosophy. | Entrepreneurship--Moral and ethical
   aspects--Philosophy.
Classification: LCC HB501 (ebook) | LCC HB501 .L628 2018 (print) | DDC
   174/.4--dc23
LC record available at https://lccn.loc.gov/2018022608

Printed in the United States of America

To the memory of my father, William Walter Livingston,
for inspiring my love of learning

To my wife, Debra Murphy,
for her unwavering support and love

And to my daughters, Florence, EmmaJean, Alexandra, and Hadley,
for being the wonderful young women they have become

Contents

Introduction

During a 1985 commencement address, Russell Kirk observed that "the most relevant things are discerned by men and women of genius in many different times and countries. . . . [and a] calm analysis of Tocqueville is more relevant to our present discontents than are the antics of the latest demagogue taken up by the mass media" (Kirk 1985, 4). Kirk also warned that those who ignore accumulated wisdom and who "immerse themselves in the mere process of this month's events become the prisoners of time and circumstance" (4). The praiseworthy entrepreneur discussed in this book is an ideal inspired by Alexis de Tocqueville's writings on honor and his observation that a democracy's definition of honor "stands for the peculiar individual character of that nation before the world" (Tocqueville 1840/1976, vol. 2, pt. 3, ch. 18).

Honorable entrepreneurs foster general human flourishing in their natural habitat, which is the extended order of peaceful social cooperation, and their virtues are revealed by a "calm analysis" spanning more than two thousand years. From the insights of Greek philosopher and scientist Aristotle, to reflections of Austrian political economist F. A. Hayek, dimensions of honorable entrepreneurship are illuminated by Roman orator, Marcus Tullius Cicero, whose writings introduced Aristotle's thinking to many of America's Founders; French political philosopher, Baron de Montesquieu, whose theories dominated discussion during America's Constitutional Convention; English writer and moralist, Samuel Johnson, whose wit and knowledge of the human condition reveal much about human foibles in the quest for happiness; and the Scottish "father of modern economics," Adam Smith, whose *Theory of Moral Sentiments* provided an essential framework for his explanation of how private interests, when pursued honorably, are a cause of the wealth of nations.

Entrepreneurs as a group flourish when they can freely engage in a competitive process while adhering to general rules of property and just conduct. The only way to achieve long-run success in a peaceful social order is to use *economic means* to win a daily market election with dollar votes being cast by consumers for their preferred products and services. Accumulating wealth using this method requires being productive and trading with others. To be successful, entrepreneurs who use *economic means* must continually search for better ways of serving others, and when they thrive there is general human flourishing. Consumers benefit from the creation of new, improved, and less costly goods, and a myriad of employment opportunities are made available that facilitate pursuit of both material and nonmaterial ends.

While the extended social order provides a fertile environment for entrepreneurs as a group, it is onerous for some who, for various reasons, cannot achieve or maintain profitability. To avoid the rigors of competition and guarantee themselves a return over cost, a few of these individuals use *political means* to gain unfair advantage conferred by political authorities. They exemplify the "the iron law of fundamental economics; . . . *man tends always to satisfy his needs and desires with the least possible exertion*" (Nock 1935/1994, 46). When it is expedient to employ *political means* to appropriate the wealth of others using the state's apparatus of compulsion and control, they rely on this method "exclusively, if possible; otherwise, in association with the *economic means*" (47).

People fortunate enough to live in an extended order of peaceful social cooperation can experience a life of "prudence, tranquility, order, and rule" (Montesquieu 1748/1977, 137), and as long as they improve their lot honorably, liberty and social progress are the natural result (Smith 1776/1981, 687). As more and more firms, commonly known as crony capitalists, expend resources in pursuit of preferential political advantage, and as other nonpreferred firms attempt to block or reverse such policies or—even worse, seek their own preferences—the social waste is immense. More significantly, principled observers begin to lose either their moral sense or their respect for the law. Because moral virtue and liberty are interdependent, and since economic freedom is a necessary condition for political freedom, crony capitalists damage the extended social order and the general human flourishing that this order makes possible.

With the growth of crony capitalism a "law of the jungle" is reemerging in which the most powerful interest groups are able to "use the guns of government to guarantee continued possession of their wealth rather than to have that continued possession contingent upon the use of that wealth in ways which best and most efficiently satisfy the needs and desires of others" (Williams 1996, 28). The honorable entrepreneur stands as a bulwark against cronyism and the human damage it causes.

The following chapters describe the origin and multiple benefits of peaceful social cooperation, and explain how crony capitalists using *political means* pose a danger to the extended social order. A resolve among current and future business leaders to avoid such practices is critical for repair of this order because: "The unit to which all things must finally be referred is not the state or humanity or any other abstraction, but the man of character. Compared with this ultimate human reality, every other reality is only a shadow in the mist" (Babbitt 1924/1979, 335–36).

The prologue presents a fictional account of a chess game with Alexis de Tocqueville, who channels himself through a contemporary entrepreneur to share his ideas about honor, and to express his concern about business practices that are legal but endangering America's freedom and prosperity. Chapter 1 then traces general rules of property and just conduct back to early Western civilization and explains why it has always been important to adhere to these rules even when doing so sometimes comes into conflict with our "natural morality."

Chapter 2 uses a Samuel Johnson fable, *The History of Rasselas: Prince of Abissinia*, to explore ideas about how happiness and wealth can be achieved by entrepreneurs as they improve the lives of others. It also touches on attributes of the extended order of peaceful social cooperation, including the relationship between economic and political freedom. Further, it points out the danger of unreflective interventionism and suggests that honorable entrepreneurs are essential for the extended social order's efficacy and, ultimately, for its survival.

Chapter 3 identifies how entrepreneurs who are honorable in the sense of Tocqueville are also virtuous in the sense of Aristotle. It discusses the practice of crony capitalism and suggests that both virtue *and* honor are barred to individuals who are astute business practitioners but who violate principles necessary for perpetuation of the extended social order. It also suggests that honorable entrepreneurs infuse soul into a discipline overly focused on science and self-interest, and that this can inspire individuals who yearn to be part of an ideal social order.

Chapter 4 extracts lessons in moral philosophy from Adam Smith's *Theory of Moral Sentiments*; describes how honorable entrepreneurs can be confused and disheartened by popular conceptions of fairness; and compares and contrasts outcomes of a spontaneous market order with "patterned" forms of social justice that are achieved using force or threat of force. Chapter 4 also touches on the importance of honor in politics; explains how honorable entrepreneurs serve as a makeweight against excessive power in America's triune social order; suggests a Credo that enumerates maxims and duties of an honorable entrepreneur; and provides an example of the power of a noble vision.

This book concludes with an epilogue in which Tocqueville returns to suggest how a shared vision of honorable entrepreneurship might be created. Examples of honor in business and politics are given that illustrate the importance for leaders in these realms to avoid a separation of the honorable and the useful.

It is hoped that this book will improve understanding of the extended order of peaceful social cooperation and its prerequisites. Entrepreneurs who pursue their self-interest honorably have the power to nurture freedom and foster general human flourishing. At the very least, each person who is honorable in the *practice* of entrepreneurship "may be sure there is one less rascal in the world" (Carlyle 1840/2006, 97).

Prologue

Playing Chess with Alexis de Tocqueville

Dear Diary: I enjoy playing chess with my friends at a small club and last week a remarkable thing happened during a game with Joe, someone I have known for twenty years. I was playing the white pieces and I opened with my usual pawn to queen four. Joe answered with his usual knight to king bishop three and after a few moves his pieces were in a Benoni-type position. We were talking about the general state of the economy and I mentioned how disturbed I was by the financial frauds being committed by people like Bernard Madoff. For three decades Madoff and a dozen of his officers operated a Ponzi scheme, and by the time he got caught in 2008 he had lost more than $17 billion entrusted to him by a wide variety of people. Many sophisticated investors, foreign banks, and charitable foundations, among others, trusted Madoff to invest their money and he squandered their funds to finance a private lifestyle that included a penthouse in Manhattan, an oceanfront mansion in the Hamptons, houses in Palm Beach, Florida, and Cap d'Antibes, France, and many other assets, including a fifty-five-foot yacht.

Joe's eyes suddenly turned dark and he began speaking with a Parisian accent. I took a break from the game and asked Bob, a mutual friend who was watching us play: "What's going on?" Bob whispered: "This has been happening periodically for several months and a psychologist treating Joe thinks that someone named Alexis from nineteenth-century France is channeling through Joe." On the eleventh move Joe played knight to rook four, which was an unusual move that I considered to be a blunder. I captured his knight with my bishop, which doubled his king rook pawns and created what I thought was a significant weakness in his king-side pawn structure.

After a couple of more moves in a game that I was certain I would win, I asked Joe to tell me his name. He answered: "My name is Tocqueville, Alexis de Tocqueville, and I am very concerned about what is now happening in America." I remembered from my college days reading about Tocqueville and his book *Democracy in America*, which my professor said is still considered one of the most insightful writings on what makes American society unique.

Joe (or was it really Tocqueville?) continued: "After departing France for New York in 1831, I spent a year traveling around America and I was able to observe and later write about the essence of American social life as well as the theory and practice of democratic government. The publication of my book brought me immediate fame in France, England, and America, and while I don't like to brag, I am still highly regarded in American college classrooms."

This voice didn't sound like Joe's but it occurred to me that Joe and Bob might be playing an elaborate trick. So I played along and asked: "Why are you here? And what is it that concerns you about American social life?" He continued and seemed prepared to talk about this subject in great detail. "I am here to warn Americans that something is undermining and weakening the creative spirit of your great country. I once said that America is great because America is good but a certain part of your goodness is being lost."

I asked him if he was talking about the Madoff scandal and his answer surprised me. "What Bernard Madoff did was immoral because he stole from others. I am more concerned about something different than this. I am referring to activities now taking place that are dishonorable even though they are considered to be perfectly legal. In my opinion, the cumulative effect of these actions will eventually dampen enterprise just as much as illegal acts of fraud and theft. Most American entrepreneurs are accomplishing great things in their economic lives but some are being dishonorable in their political lives." I continued to play along with what I still thought was a hoax and asked him to explain.

Joe looked at the board for a few minutes, moved his rook and then continued: "First, let me explain what I mean by *honor*. This is a concept that varies from country to country and from group to group within a country. People sometimes follow an unwritten code of honor even when it conflicts with religious doctrine and written law."

I moved my rook and Tocqueville continued talking as he assessed his position. "Particular groups or social classes reward the honorable acts of their members with praise, while dishonorable actions are disparaged and condemned. My studies have also revealed that specific rules of honor are only applicable to members of a group and not to outsiders. For example, in traditional societies aristocrats praised certain actions of fellow aristocrats, but they ignored the same actions of people with a lower social standing.

Conversely, behavior viewed as acceptable for commoners was sometimes considered dishonorable for members of the aristocracy."

At this point I was convinced that this was definitely not a trick. Joe is a heck of a nice guy, but as long as I have known him he has never been able to string words together as effortlessly as I was now hearing. This was obviously a learned and articulate man. I ordered two glasses of Port, which I thought was appropriate since it is sometimes referred to as the *philosopher's wine.* Being intrigued by his observations I asked: "Wasn't it once standard practice for aristocrats to fight to the death if someone tapped them on the cheek with a glove? Why would anyone consider it to be honorable to kill someone in a duel for such a small offense?"

Tocqueville moved a pawn and without looking up from the board he said: "For a group to maintain or strengthen its social standing, it is in the group's best interest to praise and encourage those practices of members that strengthen the group and to condemn behavior that weakens or undermines the group. Using honor and dishonor to allocate praise and blame respectively is one way to accomplish this. Since the feudal aristocracy was born of war and for war, courage was glorified above all other virtues. That they did not tranquilly suffer any form of insult seems silly now, but it met the needs of their military aristocracy."

I studied the board and asked: "What does all of this have to do with honor among entrepreneurs?" Tocqueville looked up and continued: "Honor in America was, in at least one respect, similar to the European medieval conception. Both ranked courage first of virtues and considered it as man's greatest moral necessity. Of course, particular actions believed to reflect courage were considerably different in the old world than they were in America." We stopped talking for a while as Tocqueville and I aggressively attacked each other's position.

After taking his bishop with my queen I asked: "What was considered to be courageous in America?" Tocqueville promptly moved his rook and replied: "In America, courage in commercial life, such as boldness in industrial undertakings, was highly regarded. In addition to entrepreneurship, the quiet virtues of honesty and hard work were generally revered and idleness was the one habit that honor was most aligned against."

Tocqueville seemed satisfied with his game, and he took a sip of Port. "As class distinctions are broken down in a democratic society," he continued, "codes of honor become less esoteric and draw continually closer to the moral laws accepted by humanity in general. This is partly due to the fact that social positions and groups in democracies are not fixed but are all jumbled together in the same constantly fluctuating crowd."

After we exchanged rooks Tocqueville said: "Honor has become much less influential in America because public opinion, which is the supreme interpreter of the law of honor, constantly fluctuates and is sometimes self-contradictory. But while democratic nations are now less influenced by no-tions of honor, each stands apart from the rest because of dominant ideas that establish actions praised as honorable or condemned as dishonorable." Toc-queville looked up from the board and spoke with a concerned look: "A democracy's definition of honor represents the peculiar individual character of that nation before the world, and in America I believe this character is changing for the worse."

After several more moves it was clear that we wouldn't be able to finish the game. It was late, and I had to oversee a project early the next day. We agreed to adjourn the game and to resume play on the following evening at seven. I normally don't like to give Joe extra time to think about his position, but Tocqueville had made some unorthodox moves and he didn't seem to be as good as Joe. Besides, I was finding it hard to concentrate on his message as well as my position on the chess board.

Dear Diary: I didn't sleep much that night. I kept wondering just how Toc-queville's ideas about honor apply to American business leaders today. I have long known that America's economic vitality depends on successful innovators, and that entrepreneurs are best able to help themselves by doing good things for others. The most successful entrepreneurs provide new and improved products, and they produce goods and services efficiently and sell them at prices people can afford to pay. The value they create for consumers does not, for the most part, result from conscious acts of altruism, but is derived as a beneficial by-product of their enlightened self-interest.

I tossed and turned and kept thinking about things I have observed throughout my business life. I have come to realize that entrepreneurs who do not produce the best possible products at the lowest possible prices will soon fail and be replaced by others who are more capable. An apple may not fall far from the tree, but the heirs of successful entrepreneurs only retain the lofty positions achieved by their forbears if they continue to employ capital for the greatest satisfaction of consumers.

I kept wondering just how all of this might relate to Tocqueville's concept of honor, and I was startled when the alarm went off at 6:00, which is the usual time I get up. I couldn't wait to learn more about Tocqueville's ideas, and as an added benefit I imagined a sequence of moves that I was pretty sure would win the game.

I returned to the club that evening and we resumed play. I made what I thought was a killer thirty-fifth move and I then asked Tocqueville: "Which actions of entrepreneurs meet the special needs of our nation and deserve praise as being honorable? And what kinds of actions are dishonorable?" Without speaking, Tocqueville studied the board for several minutes, and he then surprised me by moving his queen to his king knight's square. I had completely overlooked this possibility, and suddenly my position didn't look very strong. I moved my bishop in a feeble attempt to thwart his attack, but Tocqueville quickly threatened my king with another queen move. He then said: "A partial answer to your questions comes by examining factors that made America unique compared to other nations." I was so shocked to see that Tocqueville now had a winning position that I could barely concentrate on what he had just said. After making a few more meaningless moves in a futile position, I resigned. I learned the hard way that Tocqueville was a top-notch chess player in addition to being a profound social theorist.

I congratulated Tocqueville and we moved to two lounge chairs to continue our conversation. After recomposing myself following the surprising loss, I told him what I thought was a key element that had made America stand apart from other countries: "By protecting private property rights within a legal framework that was understandable and stable, our government helped each person to realize his private interests." Tocqueville seemed to agree with my assessment. He then handed me several pamphlets titled *Independent Reflector: On the Private and Public Virtues of an Honorable Entrepreneur*, and he said that reading them would help me understand honorable entrepreneurship and its importance for general human flourishing in America.

Dear Diary: I took the pamphlets home, spent several hours reading them, and a week later we met at the club to discuss them over several glasses of Port. I thanked Tocqueville and told him that the pamphlets helped me see how honorable entrepreneurs can be a positive force in social life that extends far beyond their contributions of material goods and services. He responded: "I'm glad you found the writings to be of value, and I hope that many more people will read them. The ancients used bronze weapons and physical force in their assaults on property. Today, dishonorable business executives commit acts of plunder when they seek and obtain preferential treatment from compliant politicians whose legislative actions weaken private property rights and undermine the Rule of Law."

Tocqueville continued: "To avoid contributing to an erosion of the principles that helped make America the envy of the world, entrepreneurs must pursue profit honorably and also praise and support the honorable actions of other entrepreneurs. When property rights are secure, long-run opportunity is enhanced for everyone. If you take this message to your fellow entrepreneurs you can help renew the creative spirit that made your country great."

I thanked Tocqueville for sharing his wisdom, and then I just had to ask: "Where did you get the idea to play knight to rook four on move eleven?" He answered: "Bobby Fischer made this same move in game three of his famous world championship match with Boris Spassky in 1972. I was there in Reykjavík, Iceland, watching that game when Fischer beat Spassky for the first time and then went on to win the match."

At this point Joe's head dipped forward. He straightened up in the chair with a puzzled look and asked: "What happened, did we finish our game?" Joe's voice had returned to his body. I smiled and said: "Yes. You won that one, and I have something really interesting to tell you."

1972 MATCH—GAME 3:
SPASSKY (WHITE); FISCHER (BLACK)

1 P-Q4, N-KB3 2 P-QB4, P-K3 3 N-KB3, P-QB4 4 P-Q5, PxP 5 PxP, P-Q3 6 N-B3, P-KN3 7 N-Q2, Q/N-Q2 8 P-K4, B-N2 9 B-K2, 0–0 10 0–0, R-K1 11 Q-B2, N-R4 12 BxN, PxB 13 N-B4, N-K4 14 N-K3, Q-R5 14 B-Q2, N-N5 15 NxN, PxN 16 B-B4, Q-B3 17 P-KN3, B-Q2 18 P-QR4, P-N3 19 K/R-K1, P-QR3 20 R-K2, P-N4 21 Q/R=K1, Q-N3 22 P-N3, R-K2 23 Q-Q3, R-N1 24 PxP, PxP 25 P-N4, P-B5 26 Q-Q2, Q/RK1 28 R-K3, P-R4 29 R/3-K2, K-R2 30 R-K3, K-N1 31 R/3-K2, BxN 32 QxB, RxP 33 RxR, RxR 34 RxR, QxR 35 B-R6, Q-N3 36 B-B1, Q-N8 37 K-B1, B-B4 38 K-K2, Q-K5ch 39 Q-K3, Q-B7ch 40 Q-Q2, Q-N6 41 Q-Q4, B-Q6ch White Resigns

Chapter One

General Rules and the Extended Social Order

Human beings living in isolation are among the world's most disadvantaged creatures because of a misalignment between our expansive wants and our limited capacity to achieve them. Other species do not experience such a wide gap between their natural desires and abilities. Ravenous and carnivorous lions, for example, have the temper, agility, and means to satiate their considerable appetites. Although sheep have none of the lion's formidable weaponry, their appetites are moderate and their food is easy to obtain. In contrast, it is extremely difficult for people living alone in the wild to survive, and small independent tribal groups can barely meet their most basic human needs (Hume 1740/1978, bk. III, pt. II, sec. II).

Before emergence of the extended order of peaceful social cooperation, primitive people living in small roving bands and tribal groups were able to survive because of their ability to accurately assess the threats and opportunities of their environment. Individuals faced significant difficulties and dangers and they were heavily dependent on members of their group for survival. Very little could be done by a person without the group's agreement or consent. Each group was generally self-reliant and actions were guided by concrete and commonly perceived aims such as acquiring adequate food and shelter. Instincts of *solidarity and altruism* inspired cooperation within a group but tribal members were instinctively aggressive toward strangers belonging to other groups (Hayek 1988, ch. 1).

EARLY FORMS OF PEACEFUL
SOCIAL COOPERATION

When primitive people provided a service, they anticipated that others would return the service and expect "another of the same kind . . . in order to maintain the same correspondence of good offices" among the parties (Hume 1740/1978, 521). In some instances, early social cooperation took the form of gift giving that was typically part of a religious ritual. The giving occurred with an expectation that there would be reciprocation involving gifts of a greater value. In the Solomon Islands, for example, each tribal leader, who was known as the *mumi* or "big man," would try to outdo the *mumi* of other tribes. The process of becoming a *mumi* required that a young man demonstrate his character by working harder than anyone else and restricting his consumption of meat and coconuts to accumulate these items for later tribal use. With help from his immediate family he would prepare a feast, and if successful he would work toward "an even greater display of generosity." This might take the form of a clubhouse constructed for his male followers and for guests to be entertained and fed (Harris 1977, 71–72).

If successive feasts attracted more tribal members willing to bring their own contributions, then tribal productivity would increase and the young man would eventually be referred to as a *mumi*. These feasts produced "a growing fabric of economic creation and exchange, with each giver hoping for greater returns but not assured of them, and with each recipient pushed to produce a further favor" (Gilder 1981, 22).

The social act of gift giving in primitive tribes was a precursor of trade in the modern era. When voluntary market transactions occur today, each side believes that he or she will be better off after the transaction than before. Traders believe that what they are getting is more valuable than what they are giving up, whether it be goods, services, or money. An unspoken dialogue at a local grocery store today might go like this: "I'll do this good thing by giving you three dollars, if you will also do something good by giving me a fresh, cold gallon of milk."

Implicit in the process of becoming a *mumi* was a tribal tradition involving property rights. A young man would have no reason to construct a clubhouse if other tribal members with superior strength could confiscate the structure for their own use or tear it down for firewood. In ancient Greece, the world's first scientific historian, Thucydides, observed that tenuous property rights slowed early development of a more widespread society. Savages did not think twice about plundering strangers for the benefit of themselves and their families or tribes. This forced people to continually move around to avoid "the violence always of some greater number." There was constant fear on land and sea, and every individual avoided accumulating a "stock of riches and planted nothing (because it was uncertain when another should invade them and carry all away)." The result was a people whose lives were miserable and who "were of no ability at all, whether for greatness of cities or other provision" (Thucydides 431 BC/1989, 2). One of the reasons that early Athens was able to flourish was that its location made it difficult for pirates to reach, and it was poor enough for them to not want to exert the required effort. Other cities along the coastline were better targets because of their wealth and accessibility.

DEVELOPMENT OF AN
EXTENDED SOCIAL ORDER

In early human history people from distant regions were unknown to each other and their cooperation was mostly indirect. For an extended social order to begin developing, savages had to form a rudimentary idea concerning probable advantages of more widespread cooperation. They had to recognize that they would be better off working together than acting as violent and deadly rivals. They probably derived this perception from the natural attachments that unite parents with each other and with their children. The visible advantages of small groups formed a basis for the idea that social groups larger than an immediate family or tribal unit might offer still greater benefits (Hume 1740/1978, bk. III, pt. II, sec. II).

As the scope of social cooperation increased, human frailty and the limitations of small tribal units were mitigated. People working together in larger groups were much more productive and they were also more secure. A growing social order facilitated material achievement through specialization of labor and trade, and members of larger social groups were better able to provide mutual comfort and support to soften the impact of bad fortune and accidents (sec. II).

For people to begin serving the diverse interests of others whom they didn't know, and to have their own interests served by strangers, traditional tribal habits of *solidarity and altruism* had to be replaced by general rules of property and contract (Hayek 1988, ch. 1). David Hume suggested three fundamental "laws of nature" that had to be embraced by primitives for the extended order of peaceful social cooperation to evolve—the stability of possession, the transference of property by consent, and the performance of promises (Hume 1740/1978, bk. III, pt. II, sec. III–V).

The stability of possession convention could only take root when each person agreed to let other people enjoy external goods acquired through their industry and good fortune without fear of plunder. This provided a "foundation for our moderation and abstinence" since it let everyone know what was his to enjoy as well as what belonged to others for their use and enjoyment (sec. III–V). Ideas of rights and obligations were not comprehensible without a concept of property, which is the constant possession of goods. Thus, as the stability of possession convention gained force, ideas of property, of right, and of obligation emerged almost simultaneously, and property became a moral convention "established by . . . the laws of justice." The obligation to defend property rights, strengthened by a belief that it was just to do so, contributed to further development of the extended social order (sec. III–V). The stability of possession convention was already well established even before the earliest history was being recorded. Since that time enterprise and economic flourishing have been closely linked to general rules of property and just conduct.

In the seventeenth century, John Locke formalized the sanctity of property in an essay "Concerning the True Original and End of Civil Government." He theorized that while resources were owned in common by human beings in their early natural state, each person has ownership in "the labor of his body, and the work of his hands" (Locke 1689/1988, bk. II, ch. V, sec. 27). When an individual removes something from its natural state and transforms it in some way by mixing the resource with his labor, he gains ownership in what was previously commonly owned. By virtue of the sweat of his brow the individual earns the right to exclude others from whatever it is he has transformed, collected, captured, or harvested. Someone who gathers acorns or picks apples from commonly owned trees gains ownership in these items, and this "makes the deer that Indian's who has killed it" (sec. 30). For Locke, this law of nature underlies property laws that have evolved "amongst those who are counted the civilized part of mankind" (sec. 30).

Manifestations of Hume's "laws of nature" that have evolved sporadically and spontaneously include private property, contract, exchange, specialization, trade, competition, and privacy. Once discovered, these economic, legal, and moral mechanisms and behaviors were passed on from generation to generation through teaching, imitation, and adherence to tradition. The extended social order prevailed because the population and wealth of groups adopting general rules of property and just conduct flourished, while groups adopting or maintaining other rules experienced atrophy and decimation (Hayek 1988, ch. 1).

With the advent of an extended social order, the way that benefits are maximized for an entire community was changed. Altruism, as it was originally practiced, meant continually giving and receiving help from known members of the tribe. In a larger society most of our actions benefit people whom we don't know. We act and exchange things because of circumstances about which we know very little, and we frequently set into motion chains of events that produce outcomes over which we have little or no control. While the good we accomplish during a normal work day is practically invisible, if we were to abandon our occupations to satisfy an instinctive desire to do good in more visible ways, general prosperity would soon be replaced by widespread poverty. We have learned that working diligently in our occupations creates more benefits for the community at large than we can produce by devoting our lives to those direct and visible acts of altruism that characterized primitive man (19). The extended social order has made it possible "to do a service to another without bearing him a real kindness" (Hume 1740/ 1978, 521).

IMPORTANCE OF GENERAL RULES
IN ANCIENT GREECE

Through the ages, stable and understandable general rules, including well-defined and enforced property rights, have been important. Social upheaval is inevitable when property is confiscated without justification beyond the power of a dominant political authority. Greek epic poet Homer illustrates this principle in the first lines of his account of the siege of Troy:

> Rage—Goddess, sing the rage of Peleus' son Achilles, murderous, doomed, that cost the Achaeans countless losses, hurling down to the House of Death so many sturdy souls, great fighters; souls, but made their bodies carrion, feasts for the dogs and birds, . . . Begin, Muse, when the two first broke and clashed (Homer 8th Cen. BC/1990, 77).

Greek supreme commander Agamemnon caused this deadly dispute when he violated the rights of lower-level tribal chieftain, Achilles. Superior power was his only justification for taking Achilles' property: "You are nothing to me . . . you [will] learn just how much greater I am than you and the next man up may shrink from matching words with me, from hoping to rival Agamemnon strength for strength" (83). It was because of this injustice that Achilles withdrew from the siege, causing general confusion, dissension, and loss of life. Homer's *Iliad* illuminates the importance of general rules before Greek city-states first created constitutions that treated private property as the primary means of achieving the ideal of freedom.

Although entrepreneurs in ancient Greece were active producers and traders, hardly anything was understood or written about them. The primary contributions of Plato, Aristotle, and other Greek intellectuals were in areas of philosophy, mathematics, geometry, and astronomy, and any economic reasoning that took place was usually intertwined with moral and political philosophy. Plato's ideal fictional city-state (the *polis*) allowed a division of labor and trade but not an accumulation of wealth, since he believed that wealth inequality resulting from commercial enterprise was a primary cause of social turmoil and tyranny. In his *Republic*, a permanent ruling caste would be assigned to regulate the economic and noneconomic activities of farmer, warrior, and artisan castes. Individuals could own property but the *polis* guardians would control its use.

Aristotle, who had been a student of Plato, viewed things differently because of his analysis of 158 extant constitutions of Greek city-states collected by his Lyceum students. By looking at each state's fundamental law, which he believed was a codification of preexisting moral habits and traditions, and then studying each state's political developments, Aristotle identified factors he considered important for political stability along with conditions apt to cause revolution.

In his comparison of good and perverted states Aristotle noted the importance of private property rights. "Property should be in a certain sense common, but, as a general rule, private; for, when everyone has a distinct interest, men will not complain of one another, and they will make more progress, because everyone will be attending to his own business" (Aristotle c. 325–323 BC/1988, vol. 1, 1263a). When he wrote "that which is common to the greatest number has the least care bestowed upon it" (1262a), Aristotle anticipated a problem known today as "tragedy of the commons"; property that is commonly owned is invariably overutilized and overexploited. In addition to economic efficiency, Aristotle also believed that private property was important for the virtue of liberality. He observed: "No one, when men have all things in common, will any longer set an example of liberality or do any liberal action; for liberality consists in the use which is made of property" (1263b). Because the virtue of generosity requires personal sacrifice, powerful political authorities of any era who confiscate and then give away *other* people's property may provide justification for doing so, but they should not be considered generous.

Even though Plato, Aristotle, and other early Greek philosophers and writers did not explain market exchange, production and trade flourished anyway because of *isonomy*, a very old legal practice described by Greek historian Herodotus as the most beautiful political order. Formally established in sixth century BC Athens by the Greek lawgiver Solon, *isonomy* predated democracy. It meant that equal laws were created for the noble and the base—all Athenian citizens were governed by known and general rules rather than by the caprice of tyrants (Hayek 1960, 164).

Aristotle developed his ideas about *isonomy* in *The Politics*, which combined his observations on politics with ideas he had previously developed on moral philosophy in *Nicomachean Ethics*. Aristotle viewed the evolution of a state as a natural consequence of man's proclivity to form associations, and he considered a well-ordered state as one that facilitates social cooperation that is required for man's most significant accomplishments. In the best states "every man, whoever he is, can act best and live happily" because the political authority rules with justice, for otherwise "there may be might where there is no right." Aristotle concluded that *isonomy*, or the Rule of

Law, is always preferable to unlimited democracy, which is the rule of man: "He who bids the law rule may be deemed to bid God and Reason alone rule, but he who bids man rule adds an element of the beast; for desire is a wild beast, and passion perverts the minds of rulers, even when they are the best of men. The law is reason unaffected by desire" (Aristotle c. 325–323 BC/ 1988, vol. 1, 1287b).

Entrepreneurship in the world's first democracy was already in decline by 431 BC when Pericles delivered his funeral oration describing Athenian freedom and contrasting it with Spartan totalitarianism. While entrepreneurs had flourished in Athens under the Rule of Law during its Golden Age, economic progress continually slowed as *isonomy* was gradually replaced by the unprincipled and unbounded lawmaking of various oligarchic and democratic political authorities. The decline continued until Phillip II of Macedonia ended Athenian democracy in 338 BC. The central idea of pure democracy is that citizens participate equally in government. While this seems to be logically consistent with *isonomy*, the Athenian experience proved otherwise. One was the Rule of Law, while the other was a tyranny of the majority.

IMPORTANCE OF GENERAL RULES IN ANCIENT ROME

In the early Roman Republic, the practice of *limitatio* that had originated with the Etruscans was adopted to foster peaceful social cooperation. Starting from a central point, surveyors used a *gramma*, which was a tool that drew perpendicular lines. These lines were used to establish boundaries of fields that were marked by stones or wooden posts known as *termini*. Each year an animal was sacrificed and its blood, mixed with incense, grain, beans, and wine, was poured into a *termini*'s hole. Anyone moving a *termini* could be killed without further justification.

The importance of property rights in ancient Rome was described by the poet Virgil. In *The Aeneid* he tells the story of a climactic fight between Aeneus, a member of the royal family of Troy who fled to Italy when Troy fell, and Turnus, king of a legendary Italian tribe known as the Rutulians. Aeneus charges toward Turnus who finds himself without a weapon. As Turnus looks about he sees "an ancient giant stone that lay at hand, by chance, upon the plain, set there as boundary mark between the fields to keep the farmers free from border quarrels" (Virgil 19 BC/1981, 346). This stone was the physical representation of a moral rule. A person's claim to a crop's yield on his parcel was considered just because he had planted, cultivated, and harvested the crop. These efforts gave individuals the right to consume or sell a crop's yield as they chose.

In ancient Rome, most intellectuals focused on history and law, and they contributed very little to an understanding of Roman business and entrepreneurship. The fortunes of economic traders were primarily advanced through development of Roman law and legal theory. One of the most important declarations of the first written Roman law, known as the Law of the Twelve Tables (451–450 BC), was that "no privileges, or statutes shall be enacted in favor of private persons, to the injury of others contrary to the law common to all citizens" (Hayek 1960, 166). The law also gave protection to owners of property. Property acquisition and possession was the subject of Table VI, while Table VII addressed rights concerning land. If property was invaded, then there was an obligation to make restitution and pay reparation for damages. In many cases, a pecuniary fine was also imposed (Gibbon 1776, ch. XLIV).

In the first century BC, Livy documented advantages that a government of law has over a government of men, and Cicero proclaimed that legislation should be constrained by general rules. Notwithstanding their insights and efforts, *isonomy* and enterprise were both in decline, and toward the end of the Roman Republic historian Sallust wrote:

> At no other time has the condition of imperial Rome been more pitiable . . . In every community those who have no means envy the good, exalt the base, hate what is old and established, long for something new, and from disgust with their own lot desire a general upheaval . . . men who were beggars and without character, and with unlimited hopes respect their country as little as they do themselves (Sallust c. 41–40 BC/1921, 63–65).

From the beginning of the Western Roman Empire to its end in 476 AD, there was a close connection between economic flourishing and political stability. Enterprise and general prosperity were sharply diminished under emperors not bound by law who exercised their power to confiscate the wealth of political opponents and others for spurious and selfish reasons. From the second century AD onward entrepreneurial activity was also impeded by rapidly advancing state socialism (Hayek 1960, 167).

Roman judges resolved many practical business problems with their opinions published as monographs. Judgments concerning property and commerce gradually accumulated and eventually became a system of law. Late in the fifth century after the fall of the Western Roman Empire, Justinian I, Emperor of Byzantium (the Eastern Roman Empire), formalized this system when he directed a codification of Roman law. During the next ten years, a commission of jurists collected and systematized laws that were still in force and the result was a comprehensive document known as the *Corpus Juris Civilis* (Body of Civil Law).

During the early Middle Ages the *Corpus Juris* fell out of use and for several hundred years emergent nation-states struggled to enforce consistent codes of law. This gap was partially filled in Western Europe by canon law, a complex set of rules developed and enforced by the Roman Church. Canon law, which was administered by "ecclesiastic courts under the jurisdiction of bishops," affected clerics, laypersons, *and* nonbelievers (Ekelund, Hebert, et. al. 1996, 63).

The Church's sacrament of penance dealt with many sins that were also secular crimes, and public penance for the sin of perjury was particularly effective in strengthening property rights and the enforcement of contracts. While perjury initially applied to dishonest dealings with the Church, it eventually came to mean any breach of contract, which most typically occurred when a debt was not paid. This change in emphasis occurred because a contract in the Middle Ages, "was almost always based on a mutual oath between the participants, sworn on some sacred object (e.g., the Scriptures or a sacred relic). Thus, the typical contract included a sacred oath that was sinful to break. Perjury *per cupiditatem* (from greed) therefore . . . referred to theft and nonpayment of valid debts" (65).

Any person who ignored or refused to pay penance assigned by the Church could be excommunicated, which was a threat that was quite effective for those who believed that the Church controlled the quality of everyone's experience after death. While alive, excommunicates were barred from all sacraments of the Church, and they believed that if they died before achieving absolution, then they would face an uncertain period in purgatory. Further, they were afraid that not seeking absolution would condemn them to an eternity in hell.

Excommunication for sins that were also violations of civil law had significant social and economic consequences even for nonbelievers. This is because many secular courts that struggled to provide temporal law found it useful to enforce provisions of excommunication (61). Excommunicates were socially ostracized, and they were constrained in the use of legal remedies, including the ability to sue. They could not enter into enforceable contracts because such documents were considered "born dead," and they could not collect outstanding debts since payments could be avoided with impunity (68).

With an increase in entrepreneurial activity throughout Europe, the *Corpus Juris* was "rediscovered" in Italy in the twelfth century and touted by religious authorities. There was an increasing need for legal forms such as contracts, and it was convenient to use the *Corpus Juris* rather than having to design entirely new systems of civil law. While *Corpus Juris* was quite useful for entrepreneurs, "Justinian with his learned professors" had elevated the power of the empire over individual freedom to enable implementation of social policy (Hayek 1960, 167). Because nothing in the *Corpus Juris* served to protect individual freedom from political authority, "it was the code of

Justinian with its conception of a prince who stood above the law that served
as the model on the Continent" (167).

THE RULE OF LAW IN ENGLAND

The Magna Carta (1215) was a seminal document that provided a foundation
stone for the English Rule of Law. The product of a struggle for power, it
gave formal protection to individual rights that had been evolving for more
than a century. Following the Battle of Hastings in 1066, William the Conqueror disarmed the English in areas of potential rebellion and expropriated
their estates. He established feudal law and divided England into seven hundred baronies that were presented to his captains. Each estate's chief tenant
shared his lands and collected duties for himself and the king, who was
initially able to confer and withdraw estates arbitrarily.

In exchange for the barons' military services a succession of kings following William granted them rights incrementally in the use of estates, and
the barons were ultimately given permission to bequeath property to their
heirs. Barons began to regard themselves as owners of the estates, and their
wealth and influence increased so much that in 1215, King John, who was
William the Conqueror's great-great grandson, was unable to evict them. In
order to force the king to sign the Magna Carta the barons needed support of
the clergy and freemen of lower social ranking. They were able to achieve
this by guaranteeing that they too would receive the same rights of property
and other rules of justice that the barons were seeking for themselves (Hume
1762/1983, ch. 11 and 455–88).

A Rule of Law evolved from the Magna Carta that sparked English entrepreneurship and economic development. It also had a profound effect on the
thinking of America's Founders. General rules in England prevented individuals from being punished and their property forfeited unless written law was
violated, as interpreted by ordinary courts following legal precedent. All
people were subject to the jurisdiction of regular courts regardless of their
rank or position in society, and no one was unfairly targeted in the law's
application.

PURE DEMOCRACY IS
NOT THE RULE OF LAW

An idea that has long been debated is whether or not democratic majorities,
or their elected representatives, should be authorized to do anything they
want to improve popular conceptions of the public good. The problem with
unbridled democracy was clearly seen by Alexis de Tocqueville who pointed
out that if a majority in its collective capacity is similar to an individual who

has opinions then it also has interests that may be contrary to those of another collective individual known as the minority.

> Now if you admit that a man vested with omnipotence can abuse it against his adversaries, why not admit the same concerning a majority? Have men, by joining together, changed their character? By becoming stronger, have they become more patient of obstacles? For my part, I cannot believe that, and I will never grant to several that power to do everything which I refuse to a single man (Tocqueville 1835/1976, 251).

In *Federalist 10*, James Madison warned:

> A pure democracy can admit of no cure for the mischief of faction. A common passion or interest will, in almost every case, be felt by a majority of the whole; . . . and there is nothing to check the inducements to sacrifice the weaker party or an obnoxious individual. Hence it is that such democracies have ever been spectacles of turbulence and contention; have ever been found incompatible with personal security or the rights of property; and have in general been as short in their lives as they have been violent in their deaths.

Later, in *Federalist 55*, he added: "In all very numerous assemblies, of whatever characters composed, passion never fails to wrest the scepter from reason. Had every Athenian citizen been a Socrates, every Athenian assembly would still have been a mob."

In his essay "On Liberty," John Stuart Mill described how the increasing popularity of democratic government throughout the world was accompanied by large-scale misunderstandings concerning the justification of authority and the role of patriots in liberty's defense. An effect of this confusion was that our resistance to tyranny was weakened. Mill viewed most of Western civilization's recorded history as a struggle between liberty and authority. In older societies, the disputants were well defined and a degree of antagonism was considered normal. On one side was the political authority, usually a king or tribal chieftain, who owed his position to conquest or inheritance. On the other side were subjects who viewed their ruler as a necessary evil— necessary for social order and protection against external enemies, but highly dangerous because of his ability to use coercive power against his subjects: "as the king of the vultures would be no less bent upon preying on the flock than any of the minor harpies, it was indispensable to be in a perpetual attitude of defense against his beak and claws." Liberty was achieved by limiting the ruler's power, and those who were committed to this task were considered patriots (Mill 1859/1989, 6).

Two methods were traditionally used to limit the power of rulers. First, the ruled exacted from the ruler recognition and acknowledgment of certain material and nonmaterial rights. If a ruler violated these political liberties, then the ruled felt justified to resist the encroachments with acts of defiance or, if necessary, by general rebellion. A second and newer method of constraining political power was to establish a constitution with consent of the ruled that limited or forbid certain types of governmental actions (6).

When the democratic form of government began to gain popularity, a false idea emerged that the interests of governors under this system would necessarily conform to the interests of the governed. Arbitrary power was believed to be checked by periodic elections, which would make representatives the people's tenants. Majority rule was thought to guarantee that rulers would not use the powers of government to advance their personal interests at the expense of the whole.

As new democracies continued to form around the globe, people were mainly concerned with the rules established for electing their representatives. They were less concerned about limiting the power of elected officials since this is only necessary when the interests of rulers are opposed to the public interest. Concentrating political power in the hands of temporary custodians was considered an effective way to help electors achieve the people's wishes. The people of a nation, so it was thought, need not worry about protecting themselves against their own will (7).

The practice of democracy, as Mill explained, revealed faults and short-comings hidden by the elegance of the romantic theorists' portrayal of this form of government. What actually happens is that "self-government" is a government of each person by all the rest; "the power of the people over themselves" is the power of some people over other people; and the "will of the people" is little more than the preferences of a majority of individuals who take the time to vote. Mill concluded that because there are always people who are eager to use the coercive power of government to oppress others, it is just as important to limit political power in a democracy as it is in any other form of government (8).

A democracy can become even more oppressive than the rule of a tyrannical king if its elected officials are not viewed as being able to represent interests contrary to the people's well-being and if they possess unconstrained political power guided by public opinion. When public opinion becomes the dominant principle used to judge the propriety of legislation, government's invasion of individual liberty penetrates deeply into every aspect of our lives. All the prejudices, superstitions, envy, jealousy, arrogance, and contemptuousness of human beings are embedded in laws invoked to do some perceived good or thwart some evil, and the eyes and ears of the people are everywhere and always on alert to detect nonapproved activities. Coercive legislation reflecting popular opinion eventually crushes the efforts and aspirations of nonconformists (12).

Bertrand de Jouvenel warned that in an unlimited democracy the general will or the will of the people "crushes each individual beneath the weight of the sum of the individuals represented by it; it oppresses each private interest in the name of a general interest which is incarnate in itself" (Jouvenel 1948/ 1993, 285).

> The history of the democratic doctrine furnishes a striking example of an intellectual system blown about by the social wind. Conceived as the foundation of liberty, it paves the way for tyranny. Born [to stand] as a bulwark against Power, it ends by providing Power with the finest soil it has ever had in which to spread itself over the social field (263).

Some practitioners of democratic tyranny adhere rigidly to custom and they believe that everyone should think and act as they do. The "self-evident" rules that they want to impose on others, however, are little more than preferences that should be given no more credence than the preferences of nonconformists. To combat this form of democratic tyranny, Mill offered a single principle that he believed is essential for a nation that values individual liberty:

> [T]he sole end for which mankind are warranted, individually or collectively, in interfering with the liberty of action of any of their number, is self-protection. The only purpose for which power can be rightfully exercised over any member of a civilized community, against his will, is to prevent harm to others. His own good, either physical or moral, is not a sufficient warrant. . . . Over himself, over his own body and mind, the individual is sovereign (Mill 1859/1989, 13).

CONSTITUTIONAL DEMOCRACY AND THE RULE OF LAW

To avoid tyranny, a political authority's power must be limited and subject to general rules of property and justice. One of the major reasons that America's Founders established a new political order was the British Parliament's 1767 declaration establishing itself as an absolute sovereign with unlimited powers. Because the British (unwritten) constitution did not check Parliament's abuses, the Founders believed it was essential to create a written and fixed constitution to circumscribe and constrain government power. They considered the Constitution to be a higher law that would diffuse power and prevent arbitrary action in any branch of government.

The conception of a superior controlling authority has taken various forms through the centuries, including natural law, God's law, and the law of pure reason. The central idea justifying a hierarchy of laws is that human intellect and moral imagination are limited. Because of this, a higher law is required to limit enactment of shortsighted and harmful legislation that may be guided by passion or a will-to-power. Thus, a limited constitutional government places long-term principles above temporary solutions to current problems. Desired ends can never justify legislative means if proposed statutes violate the fundamental law of a constitution.

John Locke's writings provided America's Founders with justification for the American Revolution and he also influenced their thinking as they drafted the Constitution. Locke believed that for a government to preserve "Lives, Liberties, and Estates," it must establish "settled, known law," consistent with nature's law; provide a "known and indifferent Judge" to adjudicate legal disputes; and provide a mechanism for enforcing judgments evenly in a timely manner (Locke 1689/1988, bk. II, ch. IX, 351). The Founders strongly believed that applying the same rules of process to everyone was essential for achieving "equality before the law." In the words of John Adams, America was to be "an empire of laws and not of men." Locke also provided the Founders with a clear definition of liberty under the law:

> Freedom of Men under Government, is, to have a standing rule to live by, common to every one of that Society, and made by the Legislative Power erected in it; A Liberty to follow my own Will in all things, where the Rule prescribes not: and not to be subject to the inconstant, uncertain, unknown, Arbitrary Will of another Man (ch. IV, 284).

In his first inaugural address, Thomas Jefferson provided his own interpretation of liberty under the law with his call for "a wise and frugal government, which shall restrain men from injuring one another, which shall leave them otherwise free to regulate their own pursuits of industry and improvement, and shall not take from the mouth of labor the bread it has earned."

Montesquieu's *Spirit of the Laws* provided guidance to the Framers concerning the doctrine of the separation of powers, and his writings advised that judges should do nothing more than be "the mouth that pronounces the words of law." The Founders were also profoundly affected by Adam Smith's *Wealth of Nations*, published in 1776. Several of them referred to it in their writings and quoted from it in their speeches. Almost everyone occupying public office at the time knew about and praised Smith's book. Smith confirmed their belief that economic development is best accomplished by individuals pursuing their self-interest in a society that limits the size and scope of government (McDonald 1985, ch. III).

From their study of history the Founders concluded that human beings are tragically flawed and vulnerable to the corrosive effects of excessive power. This darker side of human nature had been clearly displayed during the decade following the Declaration of Independence. During this time excessive corruption and demagoguery in the Continental Congress and the States resulted in a rapid deterioration of institutional safeguards that had been established for the protection of liberty and property. States continually sought to gain property at the expense of other states; the absolute authority of juries was questioned; particular churches were disestablished; and laws were passed to prevent criticism of public officials. Repeated attacks on property by Congress and the States made property less secure than it had been in the colonial period (ch. V).

What the Founders observed during this tumultuous period had been earlier seen and commented on by Niccolo Machiavelli. In the sixteenth century, Machiavelli analyzed the actions of "political man" as motivated by the will-to-power in much the same way that contemporary economists analyze "economic man" as guided by prospective profit. The core of his insights is that the study of politics is mainly a study of the struggle for power. In every era, there will be individuals who have an unbounded appetite for power, and some of them will do anything it takes inside or outside the law to achieve their ends.

Because the Founders' observations were in accord with this part of Machiavelli's writings, they heeded David Hume's warning that when a constitution is being drafted with its checks and controls, "every man ought to be supposed a knave and to have no other end in all his actions than private interests" (Hume 1742/1987b, 42). The Founders aimed to protect the ideal of liberty from unscrupulous Machiavellian political authorities by limiting the *personal* political power of public officials through the use of *impersonal* restrictions such as the Rule of Law and the Bill of Rights.

Well defined and enforced property rights are an important part of the Rule of Law. Under English common law, which provided the foundation for economic rights in early American colonies, private property is a bundle of rights that includes rights of acquisition, rights of use, and rights of transfer. Specific rights vary depending on whether property is real, intangible, or intellectual property, and a political authority that places new constraints on any part of a bundle is taking a part of that property. The partial taking of property can be a Trojan horse of tyranny if it goes mostly unnoticed, and if it creates preferential benefits for the few while causing greater harm for the many.

In addition to reducing conflicts among early Roman farmers on the Italian peninsula, and being a pillar that supports America's ideal of liberty, the demarcation of property is important for preventing a "tragedy of the commons" that inevitably occurs when property is commonly owned. Recognized as a problem by Aristotle, the deleterious effect of a common property resource is vividly illustrated by a story involving the Montagnais Indians of Quebec and Labrador who lived in the forests of the Labrador Peninsula. In the 1500s, they hunted several types of fur-bearing animals all of which were commonly owned. This worked quite well because there was a natural balance between animal and human populations. The number of animals harvested each year was small enough for the remaining animals to reproduce and sustain their populations.

This natural balance was upset in the 1600s, when French fur traders arrived. To meet the challenge of an increased demand for beaver that was rapidly diminishing its population, the Montagnais developed a system of property rights, and by the mid-1700s private hunting grounds existed in most areas where the beaver had previously been commonly owned and hunted. The Montagnais blazed family crests on trees; marked beaver houses to delineate areas that were exclusively under their control; and practiced retribution against members of other families who poached animals in violation of these rights. Because they were able to exclude nonowners from their property, they had an incentive to manage the beaver on a sustained yield basis. The Montagnais conducted sophisticated conservation practices by developing a seasonal allotment system, and by dividing their territories into quarters and harvesting beaver on each quarter-plot once every four years.

This system worked for more than a century until white trappers entered the territory and began trapping beaver indiscriminately. Because trappers didn't recognize the Montagnais' property rights, there was no longer an incentive to manage the beaver population on a sustained yield basis. Everyone began trapping this animal without constraint, and in a period of five years beaver disappeared from the Labradorean Peninsula (Smith 1981, 439–68). The "tragedy of the commons" experienced by the Montagnais Indians is present today in the form of lakes and oceans being overfished and/or overloaded with toxic waste; excessive hunting of animals in the wild for their skins, tusks and meat; and deforestation and depletion of land caused by cutting too many trees and planting too many crops.

GENERAL RULES AND THE PLIGHT
OF DEVELOPING COUNTRIES

The plight of many developing countries today reflects the absence of social conventions and mechanisms that produce general rules of property and other rights important for entrepreneurial decision making. As an example, through the late 1980s people moving from the countryside to cities in Peru were excluded from legal economic activity and neglected by an overwhelmed government. As a result, Peru experienced a rapid increase of illegal economic activity referred to by Hernando de Soto as the "informal economy." De Soto and his team of researchers at the Institute for Liberty and Democracy (ILD) found that informal economic activities were undertaken not to defy the law but to avoid starvation and accomplish socially acceptable ends such as "building a house, providing a service or developing a business" (de Soto 1989/1990, 11).

Even though the cost of working or running a business in the "informal economy" was found to be high in Peru, the cost of becoming legal in most cases was prohibitive. ILD estimated that to begin operation of a legal clothing company required two bribes (ten were solicited), eleven permits, 289 days and cost the equivalent of thirty-two months of wages; obtaining land for legal housing took an average of six years and eleven months; opening a small store took forty-three days and cost fifteen months of wages; building a legal shopping center took an average of seventeen years; and transportation services could not be started legally because the state was unwilling to award additional permits for this type of activity (134–44).

ILD also estimated costs of remaining legal in Peru, which included high taxes, compliance to excessive and sometimes arbitrary regulation, a faulty legal system, and insecure property rights. Using a sample of fifty small industrial firms, ILD found that 11.3 percent of their production costs were required to continue operating in the formal economy, and almost three-fourths of these costs were related to the administrative expense of meeting bureaucratic directives (144–48). The high cost of becoming and remaining legal in Peru caused a boom of black market activity so that by the late 1980s about half the people working in Peru were engaged in informal activities, and the value of their output was almost 40 percent of Peru's official GDP figure (12). In Peru and other countries that lack general rules of property and other individual rights, entrepreneurial innovation is mostly focused on how to avoid getting caught by the authorities. Economic development and freedom are always problematic under these conditions.

In a later study of developing nations, de Soto's ILD team found significant "informal" entrepreneurial activity even in the poorest of countries, and they estimated that people had accumulated immense savings amounting to forty times the value of aid received during the period 1945 to 1999 (de Soto 2000, 5). The problem was, and still is, that assets cannot be traded outside of small localized areas where people personally know and trust each other. This is because resources are held in defective forms. Examples include "houses built on land whose ownership rights are not adequately recorded, unincorporated businesses with undefined liability, [and] industries located where financiers and investors cannot see them" (5–6). Assets in the West provide a foundation for the creation of securities that are used as collateral for credit and that serve as a link to the owner's credit history. Because general rules of property are deficient in developing countries, their assets are little more than "dead capital" (6).

What happened in the West, and what now needs to be done in many developing countries, is that informal property was integrated into a unified formal system that is accessible to all people. Governments "must find out how and why the local conventions work" and then "build a property and capital formation system that will be recognized and enforced" (163).

In early American history, informal local rules recognized by squatters were known as "Tomahawk rights" (secured when an individual carved his initials on trees located on improved property); "Cabin rights" (people claimed land on and around cabins that they built); and "Corn rights" (land was claimed on which people grew corn crops) (116). While these early extralegal rights provoked conflict and even a threat from the Pennsylvania legislature that it would punish squatters with "pain of death," informal rights were "bought, sold, and transferred—just like official titles" (117–18). A legal innovation known as "preemption," which was eventually adopted by most states, helped solve the problem of squatter's rights and other informal property arrangements created through the nineteenth century. Preemption gave wrongful possessors the right to be compensated by official property owners for value created by their improvements. If an official property owner refused to "reimburse the squatter for these improvements, the squatter could purchase the land at a price set by a local jury" (119). Innovations comparable to preemption can provide developing countries with institutional frameworks needed for economic growth and development.

SUMMARY AND CONCLUSIONS

Entrepreneurs flourished in ancient Greece and Rome when something akin to *isonomy* prevailed. General rules provided a framework within which they were able achieve Aristotle's ideal to "act best and live happily." But *isonomy* was gradually replaced by the expanding rule of a democratic majority in ancient Greece, and was frequently suspended by powerful emperors in ancient Rome. Entrepreneurs who did their best work when general rules of property were enforced, faltered when the rule of unconstrained majorities and powerful men were predominant.

During the Constitutional Convention, America's Founders discussed the lessons of ancient Greece, Rome and later civilizations, and they referred to a large body of moral philosophy and political theory. They frequently quoted or paraphrased David Hume, James Harrington, John Locke, Montesquieu, Adam Smith, and Blackstone (McDonald 1985, ch. 1), and they recognized that freedom and general prosperity are causalities when unchecked power enables unprincipled political leaders to commit acts of plunder to punish their opponents, or to reward themselves and their friends and supporters. To prevent this, the Founders firmly believed that property should receive the same level of constitutional protection given to the most important nonmaterial rights. They were convinced that freedoms of religion and speech have little meaning unless a person can keep the fruits of his or her own efforts. James Madison wrote in the *Federalist Papers* and commented at the Constitutional Convention that political freedom can best be attained through the protection of private economic rights. Alexander Hamilton agreed and added that if you can control a man's subsistence, you can control his will.

Law, liberty, and property are inextricably linked in an extended order of peaceful social cooperation, and civilizations grow and prosper when conflict is minimized by universal rules of conduct that establish boundaries defining realms of freedom. When boundaries are clear, individuals are free to make the best use of their own knowledge in pursuit of their own ends without fear of interference. The size, structure and interconnectedness of our social order require that we not yield to our primal instincts of *solidarity and altruism* (Hayek 1988, 19). This can be difficult because the "natural morality" that united the small primitive group is still deeply ingrained in each of us, and the extended order "runs counter to some of [our] strongest instincts" (19). The situation is further complicated by the fact that we reside in "many, often overlapping, sub-orders within which old instinctual responses continue to retain some importance" (18).

The micro-cosmos (the small band or troop, or, say, our families) and the macro-cosmos (the extended order of peaceful social cooperation) are two different types of worlds and each requires its own rules. A political authority ignores lessons of history at its own peril when it attempts to apply "the unmodified, uncurbed, rules of the micro-cosmos to the macro-cosmos, as our instincts and sentimental yearnings often make us wish to do" (18). Such efforts threaten to destroy the extended social order, and extinguish the general human flourishing that this order has made possible.

Chapter Two

Pursuing Happiness and Wealth in an Extended Social Order

Ludwig von Mises observed that when people feel a sense of unease for whatever reason, they imagine how this unease can be purposefully removed, and if they believe it is possible to achieve a superior state, then they act to replace their inferior situation with another condition that they expect will produce greater happiness (Mises 1936/1981, 97). Samuel Johnson's only extended work of prose fiction, *The History of Rasselas: Prince of Abissinia*, cogently illustrates Mises's thinking for many different kinds of individuals living under varied circumstances. Published in 1759, Johnson's story revolves around Rasselas, the fourth son of a powerful emperor of Abissinia (a kingdom in northeast Africa that is now Ethiopia), a wise confidant named Imlac who serves as Rasselas' spiritual and physical guide, his sister Princess Nekayah, and her favorite servant and close friend Pekuah. Throughout Johnson's tale there are abundant insights about human aspirations and frustrations in the pursuit of happiness. He explores the unease experienced by many individuals: from those living an idyllic life in a land of lotus-eaters to others who must continually work to provide for a basic subsistence; from highly educated scholars to people whose minds "sit stupid in the gloom of perpetual vacancy"; from an old man who is close to "that hour which nature cannot long delay" to youthful revelers preoccupied with frivolous enjoyments; from social authorities occupying high political station to families of low social status living obscure and simple lives; and from traders actively engaged in market exchange to self-reliant hermits and others living secluded pastoral lives. The frustration of the fable's main characters in their pursuit of happiness illuminates the emptiness of a life dedicated exclusively to pleasure, and it shows that *living* a life is far superior to just passively experiencing it. Many of the people Rasselas encounters are unhappy either because

21

they cannot imagine an improved condition, or they lack confidence that such a state can be successfully attained. Johnson's story demonstrates why hope and human flourishing are casualties in a social order characterized by tenuous property rights and limited freedom.

HAPPINESS AND UNEASE IN
THE LAND OF LOTUS-EATERS

The story of Rasselas begins in a place of unparalleled beauty and abundance. The "happy valley" is lush with vast green meadows, all forms of exotic shrubs, plants and flowers, and a lake fed by fresh water streams lined with fruit bearing trees. There are no predators in the valley so that all grass and berry eating animals frolic and roam freely. The valley contains the "blessings of nature" while excluding its "evils," and its inhabitants are supplied with all of life's necessities. There is also an opulent palace in the valley that holds the riches of generations of Abyssinian emperors and provides its current occupants with complete security (Johnson 1759/2009, 7–9).

Rasselas, his siblings, their servants and other attendants are confined in the happy valley by his father, the emperor of Abissinia, because it is a custom for sons and daughters of Abissinian royalty to live in this place until the order of succession calls one of them to the throne. Surrounded by mountains with sole access provided by a hidden iron gate, no one can enter or leave the happy valley without the emperor's permission. Once a year the guarded gate opens to the sound of music, and the emperor enters with a variety of talented musicians and dancers. "The appearance of security and delight" provided to residents of the happy valley creates significant competition among outsiders to produce new schemes of pleasure in hopes of being chosen to permanently live in this seemingly idyllic place. During an eight-day visit the emperor grants all requests made by his children and other occupants of the valley to enhance their enjoyment and reduce the chance that they may become bored during the forthcoming year. The emperor's children experience all possible forms of pleasure and repose in the happy valley, and to further convince them of their good fortune the emperor employs sages who tell them how calamitous social life is beyond the mountains where no one can be trusted (9–10).

Most of the emperor's children are content except for Rasselas who experiences an increasing sense of unease. In his mid-twenties he begins avoiding social gatherings and he takes solitary walks in silent meditation. Instead of attending sumptuous banquets he prefers sitting under shade trees and quietly observing animal life. Everyone is puzzled by this behavior, and one of his old teachers follows him and hears him talking to himself. Rasselas mutters that while animals can quench their thirst by drinking, and can satiate their hunger by eating, he is not content with being full, and things that please him one day are not enjoyed the following day. "I can," says Rasselas, "discover within me no power of perception which is not glutted with its proper pleasure, yet I do not feel myself delighted. Man has surely some latent sense for which this place affords no gratification, or he has some desires distinct from sense which must be satisfied before he can be happy" (10–11).

During the following day the sage talks to Rasselas and points out advantages of living in the happy valley. When he asks Rasselas how it's possible to be unhappy when all wants are abundantly supplied in perfect security, Rasselas replies:

> That I want nothing or that I know not what I want, is the cause of my complaint; if I had any known want, I should have a certain wish; that wish would excite endeavor . . . But, possessing all that I can want, I find one day and one hour exactly like another, except that the latter is still more tedious than the former (12–13).

His old teacher counsels Rasselas and explains that he would value his current situation if only he could see how miserable people are outside the happy valley. Rasselas is suddenly enlivened by a desire "to see the miseries of the world, since the sight of them is necessary to happiness." For the next several months he amuses himself by pretending to be in the world he has never seen engaging in an assortment of wild adventures that always end with praiseworthy actions that detect fraud, fight oppression, or otherwise relieve distress. On one occasion he is so intent on seeking justice for an imaginary victim that he actually runs after the make-believe plunderer "with all the eagerness of real pursuit" until he is forced to stop at the foot of one of the mountains surrounding the valley. He breathlessly collects his thoughts, realizes how useless these childlike fantasies have been, and concludes that the mountains are "the fatal obstacle that hinders at once the enjoyment of pleasure, and the exercise of virtue." Rasselas now has a wish to escape the valley, and this excites an endeavor to scale or find a passageway through the mountains because he realizes that getting past the guards and opening the heavy iron gate will be impossible (13–16).

A POET'S LEARNING AND
A MEANS OF ESCAPE

Rasselas spends the next few months exploring the mountains to find a way out. His hopes of escape are dashed when he discovers that the summits are too steep to climb and that a cavern through which the lake's water discharges is full of jagged rocks with passages too narrow to traverse. Rasselas encounters an inventor who reveals that he has been secretly working on a "sailing chariot" that will enable Rasselas to fly over the mountains. After working on the machine for a full year, the project is abandoned when the inventor crashes into water during a test launch from an overhanging cliff. "His wings, which were of no use in the air, sustained him in the water, and the prince drew him to land, half dead with terror and vexation" (17–20).

Following this failed experiment, torrential rain makes it necessary for Rasselas to stay inside the palace. During this time he is intrigued by a poet, Imlac, who will later become his confidant and guide in the search for a *choice of life* that Rasselas hopes will make him happy. Imlac's poems touch on various conditions of humanity and demonstrate considerable knowledge of life outside the valley. Rasselas asks Imlac numerous questions about matters that are common to most people but unknown to the prince because of his confinement, and hoping to learn more he commands Imlac to narrate his history and explain how he came to live in the happy valley (20–21).

Imlac begins by lamenting that his life as a scholar has been to "talk in public, to think in solitude, to read and to hear, to inquire, and answer inquiries," to wander "about the world without pomp or terror," and to be unknown and unvalued by all but his fellow scholars. Rasselas learns that Imlac's father had been a successful merchant who wanted Imlac to follow in his footsteps and to eventually become the "the richest man in Abyssinia." His father gave Imlac ten thousand gold pieces and offered him the opportunity of becoming a business partner if Imlac could double the amount in four years. Despite an education that prepared him for this task, Imlac secretly despised his father's focus on accumulating wealth, and he had no intention of serving his father's wishes. Instead, he traveled extensively for the next twenty years and spent his father's money to drink "at the fountains of knowledge, to quench the thirst of curiosity" (22–24).

Early in his travels, Imlac "found that Poetry was considered as the highest learning, and regarded with a veneration somewhat approaching to that which man would pay to the Angelick Nature." Desiring to become a revered poet, he began studying and attempting to emulate the works of famous writers. Finally concluding "that no man was ever great by imitation," Imlac turned his "attention to nature and to life" to inspire his writing, and he tells Rasselas that immense knowledge is required for a poet to exhibit the "portraits of nature" and the passions of man.

Imlac describes Europeans he encountered in Palestine as "almost another order of beings." He admires their ability to obtain anything they want and he says: "a thousand arts, of which we never heard, are continually laboring for their convenience and pleasure; and whatever their own climate has denied them is supplied by their commerce." Imlac is not sure what to attribute this to but he praises their superior knowledge, and he condemns ignorance as "a vacuity in which the soul sits motionless and torpid for want of attraction" (27–32).

After passing through regions of Asia, "in the more civilized kingdoms as a trader, and among the Barbarians of the mountains as a pilgrim," Imlac finally returned home where he expected to be welcomed by his father and friends, and to delight his "old companions with the recital" of his adventures and wisdom. Imlac's hopes were soon shattered when he discovered that his father had died fourteen years earlier and had bequeathed his wealth to Imlac's brothers "who were removed to some other provinces." Most of Imlac's companions from early years had disappeared, while others could barely remember him or viewed him as "corrupted by foreign manners." Imlac attempted to open a school but was forbidden by nobles of the kingdom to teach, and his proposal to a lady who was fond of his conversation was rejected because his father had been a merchant. Wearied by these disappointments, Imlac resolved to hide himself from the world, "and depend no longer on the opinion or caprice of others." When the opportunity presented itself, he bid "farewell to hope and fear" and resigned himself "with joy to perpetual confinement" in the happy valley (32–33).

When Rasselas asks if he found happiness in the valley, Imlac responds: "I know not one of all your attendants who does not lament the hour when he entered this retreat." Imlac tells Rasselas that he is probably less unhappy than most because of his considerable experiences and memories, which he "can vary and combine at pleasure." Imlac points out that the only people in the valley who seem to be completely at ease are those "whose minds have no impression but of the present moment, are either corroded by malignant passions, or sit stupid in the gloom of perpetual vacancy." He also observes: "There may be community of material possessions, but there can never be community of love or of esteem." Some individuals will always be more pleasing than others, and "he that knows himself despised will always be envious; and still more envious and malevolent, if he is condemned to live in the presence of those who despise him" (34).

Rasselas confesses to Imlac that he has long wanted to leave the valley in order to deliberately make his *choice of life*. Imlac agrees to help Rasselas escape but warns that "The world, which you figure to yourself smooth and quiet as the lake in the valley, you will find a sea foaming with tempests, and boiling with whirlpools: you will be sometimes overwhelmed by the waves of violence, and sometimes dashed against the rocks of treachery" (35).

When the rainy season ends, Rasselas and Imlac discover parts of the mountain that have been washed away. They find a "small cavern, concealed by a thicket," and over a period of several days they dig their way through the mountain to daylight. As they plan their final escape they learn that Rasselas' favorite sister, princess Nekayah, has been secretly watching them. She is "equally weary of confinement," and wants to leave the valley with Rasselas and Imlac. They make plans and gather "jewels sufficient to make them rich whenever they come into a place of commerce." During the next

night of a full moon, Rasselas, Imlac, Nekayah and her favorite maid Pekuah
make their way through the mountain's hidden cavern and they strike out on
an adventure to discover how life can be lived and whether or not happiness
can be found outside the happy valley (35–39).

UNEASE OUTSIDE OF THE HAPPY VALLEY

Rasselas and Nekayah are nervous and uncertain about how to conduct themselves, and Imlac helps with this transition by taking them to Cairo where
they spend two years learning the local customs and language. Imlac believes
that Cairo is a city that will give Rasselas an opportunity to learn about "the
various ranks and conditions of mankind" from which he can make a *choice
of life* that most suits him. Rasselas is perplexed that everyone he sees seems
to be happy while his own mind remains restless and uneasy. Imlac comforts
him with an observation: "Every man may, by examining his own mind,
guess what passes in the minds of others: when you feel that your own gaiety
is counterfeit, it may justly lead you to suspect that of your companions not
to be sincere." Moreover, Imlac points out that unease for some is unremitting: "Every man is placed in his present condition by causes which acted
without his foresight, and with which he did not always willingly cooperate."
Thus, hardly anyone "does not think the lot of his neighbor better than his
own" (40–43).

Believing that his wealth can help him avoid the human foibles described
by Imlac, Rasselas eventually begins his quest to survey the world and make
a *choice of life* that will produce happiness. His first experiment is to visit
and observe "young men of spirit and gaiety" whose primary interests are "to
gratify their desires" and who spend all their time "in a succession of enjoyments." Rasselas becomes "weary and disgusted" after a few days when he
finds their "laughter without motive" and their pleasures "gross and sensual."
Before continuing his search for a *choice of life*, Rasselas advises the young
men: "Perpetual levity must end in ignorance; and intemperance, though it
may fire the spirits for an hour, will make life short or miserable." They
respond by staring at him in silence and then driving him away with a
"general chorus of continued laughter" (43–44).

Rasselas next encounters a Stoic philosopher who discourses "with great
energy on the government of the passions. His look is venerable, his action
graceful, his pronunciation clear, and his diction elegant." He compares "reason to the sun, of which the light is constant, uniform, and lasting; and fancy
to a meteor, of bright but transitory luster, irregular in its motion, and delusive in its direction." Rasselas tells Imlac that this is a man whose life is
worthy of emulation, and that happiness is sure to come to those who look
with "indifference on those modes or accidents to which the vulgar give the

names of good and evil," and who "arm themselves against the shafts of malice or misfortune, by invulnerable patience." Imlac warns Rasselas that teachers of morality "discourse like angels, but they live like men." The wisdom of this observation is soon made visible when the philosopher withdraws himself from social life because of his daughter's untimely death. Rasselas discovers that "wisdom has no strength to arm the heart against calamity," and he continues his search elsewhere for a *choice of life* "convinced of the emptiness of rhetorical sound, and the efficacy of polished periods and studied sentences" (44–46).

Rasselas decides to visit a venerable hermit who lives on the Nile several hundred miles from Cairo to determine if "felicity, not found in public life can be found in solitude" and whether an older and virtuous man can teach him "any peculiar art of shunning evils, or enduring them." During the journey, accompanied by Imlac and Nekayah, Rasselas passes through an area where shepherds are tending their flocks with lambs playing in the fields. Imlac suggests that because this is a life often celebrated by poets and other writers "for its innocence and quiet" they should visit the shepherds in their tents to see if the search for a *choice of life* can be concluded in "pastoral simplicity." They are surprised to find people "so rude and ignorant, so little able to compare the good with the evil of the occupation, and so indistinct in their narratives and descriptions, that very little could be learned from them." The shepherds' hearts seem to be permanently "cankered with discontent" because they feel "condemned to labor for the luxury of the rich" (46–47).

On the third day of their journey they reach the hermit who lives comfortably in a multi-roomed cavern in the side of a mountain, and he offers them food and a place to stay for the night. When he is asked for advice about a *choice of life*, the hermit replies that every form of life is good if we can remove ourselves "from all apparent evil." The hermit relates that he began living alone fifteen years earlier because of his disappointment as a soldier at being passed over for a promotion that was given to a younger less able officer. At the beginning of his retreat he "rejoiced like a tempest-beaten sailor at his entrance into the harbor" but once the novelty wore off he became "unsettled and distracted," and while his solitude enabled him to "escape the example of bad men" he also gave up "the counsel and conversation of the good." Lamenting his inability to remove himself from vice without also "retiring from the exercise of virtue" the hermit informs Rasselas that he is ready to return to civilization and he joins Rasselas, Imlac, and Nekayah on their return trip to Cairo (49–51).

Rasselas next joins "an assembly of learned men," who regularly meet "to unbend their minds, and compare their opinions." One topic of conversation is the hermit's return to Cairo. A member of the group predicts that the hermit will likely resume his isolated existence, and then later return to Cairo again if still alive and unrestrained by shame. He observes that our hope of happiness is so powerful that experiences producing misery are painted by the imagination as desirable when viewed at a sufficient distance. Another conversation is begun by a philosopher who instructs the assembly: "The way to be happy is to live according to nature, in obedience to that universal and unalterable law with which every heart is originally impressed; which is not written on it by precept, but engraved by destiny, not instilled by education, but infused at our nativity." Following the philosopher's loquacious monologue about the virtues of living according to nature and his obscure answer to a question asking what this means, Rasselas concludes that nothing more can be gained from these sages who frequently become more confusing the longer they talk (51–53).

Rasselas and his sister hatch a plan to divide their experiments: Rasselas will explore "the splendor of courts," while Nekayah will focus on learning about the "shades of humbler life." Rasselas expects to find that happiness is felt by kings who are "approached with reverence, and heard with obedience," and who have the power to extend their "edicts to a whole kingdom." He imagines that there surely can be no pleasure exceeding that produced by "thousands all made happy by wise administration." Rasselas surprisingly finds the lives of individuals occupying high stations to be "a continual succession of plots and detections, stratagems and escapes, faction and treachery." All those in power that he studies are either carried away in chains or murdered (54–55).

For her part, Nekayah finds people whose thoughts are narrow, whose wishes are low, and whose "merriment often artificial. Their pleasures, poor as they are, cannot be preserved pure, but are embittered by petty competitions and worthless emulation." Many seem to love triflers like themselves, and their affections are "seldom fixed on sense or virtue, and therefore seldom end but in vexation." Their grief and their joy are transient and their minds are "unconnected with the past or future, so that one desire easily gives way to another." Rasselas and Nekayah conclude that happiness is not to be found either in lowly private homes or in the high courts of political authorities (55–56), and they agree that "visible happiness" is not always found "in proportion to visible virtue. All natural and almost all political evils, are incident alike to the bad and good." The benefits of virtue are "quietness of conscience, [and the] steady prospect of a happier state . . . [both of which] may enable us to endure calamity with patience" (60–61).

At this point, a discouraged Rasselas is tempted to end his search for a life that might make him happy. Imlac suggests that a fruitful diversion from their disappointing quest will be to visit the pyramids, which may help them gain perspective: "To judge rightly of the present we must oppose it to the past; for all judgment is comparative, and of the future nothing can be known" (67). During their travel to the pyramids Imlac, Rasselas, Nekayah, and Pekuah experience a calamity when Pekuah is kidnapped and held for ransom. Following an unsuccessful search for Pekuah, Rasselas and the others return to Cairo. They are later able to secure Pekuah's return by paying a ransom, and following a happy reunion, Nekayah and Rasselas resume their search in Cairo for a *choice of life* (69–73).

Rasselas has learned much since leaving the happy valley and he informs Imlac that he has decided "to devote himself to science, and pass the rest of his days in literary solitude." Imlac warns Rasselas that before making this *choice of life* he needs to be aware of its hazards and he arranges for Rasselas to visit a renowned astronomer "who has spent forty years in unwearied attention to the motions and appearances of the celestial bodies, and has drawn out his soul in endless calculations." Notwithstanding his vast comprehension, capacious memory, integrity and benevolence, the astronomer is clearly experiencing a sense of unease. Imlac soon discovers that its cause is the astronomer's belief that he can control the weather, and he worries about how this can be done justly, since mistakes in the distribution of rain and sunshine can wreak havoc around the globe. Imlac explains to Rasselas that the astronomer's delusion is not uncommon when imagination predominates over reason. "To indulge the power of fiction, and send imagination out upon the wing, is often the sport of those who delight too much in silent speculation." Further, Imlac warns: "Of the uncertainties of our present state, the most dreadful and alarming is the uncertain continuance of reason." The intellectual who fixates on a favorite conception, and who "feasts" on its "luscious falsehood" even when "offended with the bitterness of truth," eventually begins to regard fiction as reality. When "false opinions fasten upon the mind, life passes in dreams of rapture or of anguish" (88–94).

During an evening when Rasselas and his sister are walking along the bank of the Nile they spot an old man that Rasselas remembers from the assembly of sages. They are curious to ask this person, "whose years have calmed his passions, but not clouded his reason," if it is youth alone that struggles with vexation, "and whether any better hope remains for the latter part of life." Rasselas and his sister are soon disappointed by the man who complains about the pains he has suffered from the "vicissitudes of life"; the irrelevance of praise that he can no longer share with his friends and relatives who are dead; the uselessness of riches and tedium of employment near the end of his life; the regret of "time squandered upon trifles, and more lost in idleness and vacancy"; and of the many opportunities of accomplishing good that were left unstarted and the many more that were never finished. As he departs, the old man says that he is eager for the "hour which nature cannot long delay" so that he can "possess in a better state" the happiness he wasn't able to find and the virtue he never attained. Unsurprisingly, the old man leaves Rasselas and Nekayah "not much elated with the hope of long life" (95–97).

Johnson concludes his story with Rasselas and his sister comparing "the different forms of life which they had observed, and with various schemes of happiness which each of them had formed." The princess was most impressed with people they encountered who possessed knowledge, and she imagines becoming a scientist and then founding a college of learned women to communicate wisdom, "and raise up for the next age models of prudence, and patterns of piety." Rasselas imagines administering justice in a little kingdom, although he isn't sure how this can be done, and he can't decide on "the limits of his dominion" or "the number of his subjects." Rasselas and Nekayah, both realizing that these dreams can never be achieved, decide to depart Cairo and return to Abissinia (108).

THE EXPERIENCE MACHINE
AND HAPPINESS IN CAIRO

The physical pleasure Rasselas experienced in the happy valley wasn't enough to make him happy. The philosopher Robert Nozick illuminates the emptiness of a life dedicated exclusively to experiencing pleasure (Nozick 1974, 42–45). He wonders what might happen if an individual could experience a false reality by floating in a tank of liquid and plugging into an "experience machine." With electrodes connected to his or her brain, each person would be able to choose any of life's many experiences from a catalog, and could periodically unplug and leave the tank to decide whether or not to continue a current experience or to plug into a new one. Pleasures provided by the experience machine would be completely realistic so that once people are plugged in they would have no idea that they are floating in a tank. People would grow old in the tank, and they would eventually die.

Nozick suspects that most people, if given this opportunity, would not want to spend their lives plugged into such a machine or into any other hypothetical machine such as a transformation machine to change us into the kind of person we want to be, or a result machine to create a world of our choosing and place us in it as we might want. People would reject using these machines to live their lives because they would want to "do certain things, and not just have the experience of doing them," and they would want to "*be* a certain way," and to make themselves the kind of person they want to be (43–44).

The happy valley was Rasselas's experience machine. He was unhappy because he was not free to discover a reality deeper than the artificial world created by his father. The futile attempts of Rasselas to achieve happiness by pretending to engage in virtuous activities were also doomed to fail. As Aristotle observed, we only acquire moral virtues by actually exercising them. Just as "men become builders by building and lyre players by playing the lyre; so too we become just by doing just acts, temperate by doing temperate acts, brave by doing brave acts" (Aristotle c. 340 BC/1973, bk. II, ch. 1, 369, 1103a–b).

Rasselas wasn't free in the happy valley to pursue and discover his own happiness, and events following his escape showed that freedom alone was not enough to make him happy. If exercising virtues of character can produce happiness, as Aristotle believed, then the lives of people outside the valley seemed empty to Rasselas because he and his sister were passively observing and not living them. Experiencing life vicariously can be as barren as being connected to one of Nozick's machines.

Through all of his travels, Rasselas only once observed people "from all the corners of the earth" who seemed to be truly happy. They were merchants "of every character and every occupation" who were attracted to Cairo because commerce there was considered honorable. Everywhere Rasselas went in Cairo he found "gayety and kindness." Cairo seemed to overflow "with universal plenty," and nothing was "withheld either from want or merit." Gold and silver coins were freely exchanged by traders, and there was much giving in Cairo because "every heart" melted "with benevolence" (Johnson 1759/2009, 40–41). Although Imlac warned Rasselas that his perception of this general happiness in Cairo may not have been entirely accurate, the city's radiant environment provides a window into how traders who are free and secure enough to use their own means to pursuit their private ends can achieve both wealth *and* happiness while contributing to the social good.

ACHIEVING WEALTH *AND* HAPPINESS

In the entirety of Johnson's story, it is the possession of wealth rather than its accumulation that invariably produces a sense of unease. A wealthy Rasselas was unhappy living in a place of unparalleled beauty, abundance, and security, and a well-funded Imlac traveled and drank "at the fountains of knowledge" only to retire in despair "to perpetual confinement" inside the valley's guarded iron gates. Imlac's father was "honest, frugal and diligent" in his acquisition of wealth, but once he became rich he was forced to spend considerable time and energy concealing it from province governors intent on plundering his holdings (22). A final example is provided by a rich man encountered by Rasselas and his companions outside of Cairo on their way to see the hermit. He lives in "a stately palace built upon a hill surrounded with woods," and when Rasselas comments about how cheerful people seem to be who are living on the estate, the man replies that "appearances are delusive. My prosperity puts my life in danger; the Bassa of Egypt is my enemy, incensed only by my wealth and popularity." The man informs Rasselas that the protection he is receiving from "princes of the country" is tenuous, and

that "as the favor of the great is uncertain, I know not how soon my defend-
ers may be persuaded to share the plunder with the Bassa." Rasselas learns
that much of the man's accumulated treasure has already been moved to
another country and he is fully prepared to evacuate his mansion and gardens
for his enemies to despoil (47–48).

While Johnson's tale describes the unease associated with protecting accumulated wealth when property rights are tenuous, Adam Smith's parable
of the poor man's son warns that onerous sacrifices are sometimes made to
acquire wealth. In *The Theory of Moral Sentiments*, published the same year
as Johnson's *History of Rasselas*, Smith suggests that a life-long obsessive
pursuit of wealth can produce material well-being but can also leave a person
exhausted and miserable. The poor man's son "whom heaven in its anger has
visited with ambition," finds inadequate everything about his condition and
he admires everything about being rich.

> He finds the cottage of his father too small for his accommodation, and fancies
> he should be lodged more at his ease in a palace. He is displeased with being
> obliged to walk a-foot, or to endure the fatigue of riding on horseback. He sees
> his superiors carried about in machines, and imagines that in one of these he
> could travel with less inconveniency . . . He is enchanted with the distant idea
> of this felicity (Smith 1759/1982, 181).

To accumulate wealth the poor man's son labors relentlessly to acquire the
needed education that he uses during long hours and countless years that
leaves barely enough time for sleep. "Through the whole of his life he pursues the idea of a certain artificial and elegant repose which he may never
arrive at," and "in the last dregs of [his] life, his body [is] wasted with toil
and diseases, [and] his mind [is] galled and ruffled by the memory of a
thousand injuries and disappointments which he imagines he has met with
from the injustice of his enemies, or from the perfidy and ingratitude of his
friends." He realizes too late that he has sacrificed real tranquility for ends
that are "mere trinkets of frivolous utility" (181).

For Smith, the unease of individuals who feel compelled to pursue riches
is caused by a deception of overrating the benefits of wealth compared to
being poor (149). While this is socially beneficial in that it "rouses and keeps
in continual motion the industry of mankind" (183), real happiness is produced by a clear conscience, good health, and freedom from debt, which the
poor can easily enjoy. Smith even suggests that "the beggar, who suns himself by the side of the highway, possesses that security which kings are
fighting for" (185).

Smith provides insight into how an entrepreneur can avoid the misery
experienced by the poor man's son. His advice is to exercise "superior prudence," which is "the best head joined with the best heart." The virtue of
regular prudence is "The care of the health, of the fortune, of the rank and

reputation of the individual, the objects upon which his comfort and happiness in this life are supposed principally to depend" (213). Superior prudence is "directed to greater and nobler purposes." It is regular prudence "combined with many greater and more splendid virtues, with valour, with extensive and strong benevolence, with a sacred regard to the rules of justice, and all these supported by a proper degree of self-command" (216).

While business success and wealth accumulation are associated with making use of regular prudence to meet the most strongly felt needs of customers, honorable entrepreneurs who choose not to live the life of a miser are guided by a constellation of nonmaterial and altruistic interests. Their happiness is produced by an enlightened self-interest informed by scientific and artistic interests, and animated by a fellow feeling described thusly by Smith: "How selfish soever man may be supposed, there are evidently some principles in his nature, which interest him in the fortune of others, and render their happiness necessary to him, though he derives nothing from it except the pleasure of seeing it" (9).

LIVING THE LIFE OF AN ENTREPRENEUR

The word "entrepreneur" was coined in 1800 by French economist J. B. Say, who defined the entrepreneur as someone who "shifts economic resources out of an area of lower and into an area of higher productivity and greater yield." The fruits of entrepreneurship were realized long before the beginning of recorded history. There is evidence of long-distance trade occurring more than one hundred thousand years ago during the Middle Paleolithic Age. Homer's poetic account of Odysseus's return home following the destruction of Troy makes reference to active networks of trade in the Mediterranean as early as the thirteenth century BC. The goddess Athena is described as traveling from Mount Olympus to speak with Odysseus's son, Telemachus, and she avoids detection by disguising herself as a merchant with a shipload of iron to be traded for bronze.

Early commercial life in ancient Greece was mostly agricultural. Important crops were grain milled into flour to produce biscuits, cakes, and pastries; grapes to make raisins and wine; and olives to provide oil for food, lighting fuel, and skin conditioner. Coastal fishermen kept local markets stocked with fresh fish; salt was obtained by evaporating seawater in shallow lagoons; and tanneries supplied leather for shoes, shields, harnesses, and saddles. There were also extractive industries that provided marble and limestone for buildings and sculpture, and that mined ores for gold, silver, copper, and iron.

Other businesses fabricated wood for houses, furniture, boats, and carts; constructed public buildings and monuments; prepared gold and silver for decorative objects and jewelry; and cast bronze for tableware and weapons. Artisans made jewelry, produced glass bowls, and created ceramic vases and lamps. Traveling by ship took Greek entrepreneurs only about a day to reach prime markets, and Greek culture spread rapidly around the Mediterranean because of heavy trading and the development of colonies along major shipping routes (Starr 1971a).

Agriculture was also the primary source of production during the early Roman Republic (509–338 BC). The importance of agriculture was reflected by "Roman proper names such as Cicero (chick pea) and Fabius (bean) . . . *Sincerus* originally was a description of honey, and was used to indicate 'without wax;' and *egregious* was a sheep 'not in the herd'" (Starr 1971b, 47). Long-distance trade during this period was primarily carried out by Patricians who were the wealthiest families in the early Roman Republic. The harvests derived from their significant land holdings were taken care of by cheap slave labor and were shipped and traded along established routes on land and sea created by conquest and alliance. Wine was a particularly lucrative export during this period. As was true in Greece, agricultural exports stimulated development of other markets and the production of trade-related items such as clay containers, ships, and wagons.

After 338 BC, a series of military successes and rapidly expanding trade routes significantly increased both entrepreneurial opportunity and Rome's political power on the Italian peninsula. *Lex Claudia*, passed in 218 BC, restricted commercial activities that Roman Senators and their sons could conduct because money lending and trading as middlemen were considered vulgar and beneath their social status. *Lex Claudia* reduced competition in these and other areas of commerce as the Senators focused on large-scale farming. This enabled the equestrian order, which was a lower aristocratic class, to become wealthy more rapidly by moving into mining and other industries that produced highly profitable exportable items. For hundreds of years until the end of the Western Roman Empire in 476 AD, economic growth and entrepreneurial opportunity were closely linked to the opening of new trade routes and the evolution of Roman commercial law.

Throughout history entrepreneurs have solved multiple social crises and created many useful innovations. At times they have done this by transforming unknown or underutilized resources into more useable and productive forms. For example, in the fourteenth century BC, iron and bronze were equally suited for uses being made of these metals, although bronze was preferred because iron cost several thousand times more to produce. Constant squabbling among Mediterranean city-states resulted in the collapse of trade and a reduced supply of tin, a Greek import necessary for bronze production. When Achaean bronze prices soared because of a shortage of this essential resource, entrepreneurs hoping to profit from this situation began a search for less expensive ways of producing iron. A lengthy trial-and-error process spanning several hundred years finally resulted in a seventh century BC technological breakthrough that reduced iron prices to about one-tenth of the cost of bronze. The entrepreneurial objective of reducing cost smoothed passage in this part of the world from the Bronze Age to the Iron Age.

In sixteenth-century England, entrepreneurs began looking for new resources because of rising wood prices due to rapid population growth, economic expansion, and commercial and military shipbuilding. Because technology favored wood use, entrepreneurs had to conduct many experiments using coal before they determined how it could be used as a viable and low cost wood substitute. The commercial success of coal created a new and abundant resource that fueled England's economic expansion during the eighteenth and nineteenth centuries.

In America, entrepreneurs pursuing profit led the transition from wood to coal during the nineteenth century, and they also discovered a new resource by making use of something that had previously been considered a nuisance. This particular discovery was stimulated by whale oil prices that increased by over 600 percent from 1832 to 1865 because of the Confederacy's use of whale oil ships to transport war supplies. Many people could no longer afford to use whale oil as fuel for their lamps, and when entrepreneurs set out to find a lower cost alternative they found it in the form of kerosene. People were provided a cheap source of illumination using a substance that had previously been burned off the surface of oil pools.

Sometimes purposeful entrepreneurs are simply trying to solve challenges impeding their introduction of new or improved products. Cyrus McCormick, for example, improved the design of a mechanical reaper that had originally been developed by his father. Farmers in the 1830s harvested wheat mainly by hand using a scythe, and for a period of about two weeks each year they needed help from their friends and neighbors to cut the stalks and bundle them into shocks ready for threshing. Beyond this narrow time frame the maturing wheat would become too heavy and bend to the ground making collection of the grain impossible. It was clear that the productivity of a harvest could be significantly increased if a dependable machine were available to speed up the slow labor intensive process.

McCormick sold such a machine, which "could cut fifteen or twenty acres per day where a man with a scythe could do two or, at most, two and a half" (Gunderson 1989, 93). After building a production facility in Chicago that was close to his customer base, McCormick was the first in his industry to develop interchangeable parts that could be used along his production line. The improved efficiency of this innovation enabled him to sell his mechanical reaper for around $150, which was half the price of competitive reapers. The problem was that the average farmer who cut wheat by hand didn't earn enough to buy the machine. The farmer could only afford it by being more productive and earning a higher income that was only possible using the machine. McCormick solved this classic catch-22 problem by being one of the first manufacturers in America to offer installment credit to his customers. For a down payment of about a third of the purchase price, a farmer could acquire the mechanical reaper and then later pay the balance from increased revenue created by using the machine.

Innovations by entrepreneurs occur every day in a discovery process going on throughout America's extended social order. In the area of communications there has been a transformation from the early use of carrier pigeons and smoke signals, to mail delivered by horse, to the use of the telegraph beginning with Samuel Morse's Washington-to-Baltimore transmission in 1844. Next came the telephone, Telex, and fax, and now there are the internet and latest smartphones. In medicine, practices and products on the horizon include genetic testing to determine an individual's risk of disease and therapies that are likely to work best; therapeutic vaccines that will use the body's immune system to treat Alzheimer's, hepatitis, multiple sclerosis, and rheumatoid arthritis; regenerative medicine that will grow replacement body parts, including livers, kidneys, pancreases, and hearts; nanoparticle drug delivery that will release controlled amounts of potent chemicals that can target and affect only diseased tissue; computerized implants that will dole out drugs for as long as a year and that respond to a patient's body chemistry to adjust doses as needed; an electronic "eye" with a computer chip that will transmit images to the brain to provide the blind with rudimentary vision; and super-imaging that will detect disease at the cellular or molecular level and enable surgeons during an operation to see through blood and tissue.

THE EXTENDED ORDER OF
PEACEFUL SOCIAL COOPERATION

The entrepreneur now plays an essential role in the peaceful coordination of economic activities of large numbers of people spanning the globe. This is demonstrated in "I, Pencil," a story told by Leonard E. Read who assumes the voice of an ordinary lead pencil (Read 1958). Read begins his story by saying "*not a single person on the face of this earth knows how to make me.*" He then supports this claim by describing all of the resources and processes that go into the making of a pencil. Harvesting and shipping trees to a mill involve many antecedent processes required to make the saws, axes, ropes, motors, flatcars, rails, logging camps, mess halls, and even the coffee that the loggers drink. The conversion of the logs to pencil size slats is a similarly intricate process, as is the creation of the lead (which is actually chemicals mixed with graphite from Ceylon and clay from Mississippi that is baked at almost two thousand degrees Fahrenheit); the production of brass and its rings of black nickel that holds the eraser; the transformation of Indonesian rapeseed oil and a complex chemical compound using rubber as a binding agent that shapes and colors the eraser; the numerous other processes required to assemble all of the pencil's component parts; and the final painting and labeling that uses six coats of yellow lacquer covered by "a film formed by applying heat to carbon black mixed with resins."

Read's account of how the pencil is created clearly demonstrates that not one person among the tens of thousands who were involved in this process could understand, let alone perform all of the required tasks. Most contributed only a very small amount of knowledge and service in the pencil's creation. They were engaged in this multifaceted creation of a pencil not because they wanted one (some wouldn't know what to do with a pencil), but because "[e]ach saw his work as a way to get the goods and services he wanted" that were produced by others who did so with the intent of buying a pencil (Friedman and Friedman 1980, 12).

Entrepreneurs who directed and oversaw work in the multiple pencil-related businesses were not carrying out the orders of a supreme pencil authority. "These people live in many lands, speak different languages, practice different religions, may even hate one another—yet none of these differences prevented them from cooperating to produce a pencil" (13). What occurs in the extended market order is a social alchemy in which the various trading partners believe that the transactions will make them better off. Voluntary exchange does not take place unless all parties expect to benefit. Entrepreneurs are guided to accept various business arrangements by prices and anticipated profits rather than by the nationality, ethnicity, political belief and other nonmarket attributes of trading partners that can be a source of enmity and conflict. "As a result, the price system enables people to cooperate peacefully in one phase of their life while each one goes about his own business in respect of everything else" (13).

Services received by people who "go about their own business" in the extended social order far exceed services that they provide. Consider, for example, a physician living in Sri Lanka (formerly Ceylon) who provides services to many patients, including miners of graphite used for pencils. He does this to obtain "certificates" to claim services of many others at a time, place, and form of his choosing (Bastiat 1850a/1964, 5). If he decides to transfer certificates to his son who is studying architecture in the United States, then the certificates can be used to obtain multiple services from people responsible for his son's lodging, food, clothing, books, instruction, and many other items. These and most other services provided every day in the extended order are traded for "distant and past services," and a full settlement of the Sri Lankan physician's toil may not be achieved until his son has used the certificates to earn a degree in architecture.

Each person in the extended social order has the power "to set in motion men of all lands, all races" and of times both past and future (5). The physician's son is able to receive a myriad of services from a multitude of people, because his father gave medical care to patients in the past who acquired certificates for care by providing their own services in the more distant past. The physician's patients as well as the people they served most likely have nothing "in common with those whose labor is being performed" for the benefit of his son (6). The global web connecting services provided and received by people across generations who are mostly unknown to each other is incredibly complex, mostly invisible, and is one of the world's unappreciated marvels.

In our modern society with its extensive division of labor and widely dispersed information, profit or loss is how entrepreneurs are informed of changing consumer preferences. Similarly, prospective profit also guides entrepreneurs in their selection of inputs to produce goods most efficiently. Production costs in America can be affected by many factors, such as weather conditions in Brazil, changing labor laws in Japan, and new technologies in Canada. These and many other circumstances are made known to producers in the form of changing resource prices. A forest fire in Canada, for example, will increase the price of a certain kind of wood, and in order to avoid a decline in profit, pencil producers will substitute a relatively abundant and inexpensive resource for the more costly wood. This focus on efficiency is socially desirable because pencil entrepreneurs are conserving a wood resource that is now relatively scarce.

Because resources have multiple alternative uses, it's important that entrepreneurs who provide resources and intermediate products to those who make pencils and paper and many other products are guided by prices and prospective profits. A surge in the demand for paper and decline in demand for pencils will change prospective profits for these two products and give resource owners an incentive to move from the pencil to the paper industry. It's only possible for the aforementioned adjustments in product and resource markets to occur when property is privately owned, and prices, profits and losses are allowed to vary without interference of a political authority. An economic system without these attributes is chaotic with "unbalanced and unmatched production, shortages of this and unusable surpluses of that, duplications, bottlenecks, time lags, inefficiency, and appalling waste" (Hazlitt 1971/1993, 246).

The only alternative to profit as a guiding mechanism for production is the use of quotas, and regardless of how the planning committee defines a quota, results are usually perverse. In the Soviet Union, for example, "when Soviet nail factories had their output measured by weight, they tended to make big, heavy nails, even if many of these big nails sat unsold on the shelves while the country was 'crying for small nails'" (Sowell 1980, 215). Additionally, when quotas were defined in units of *gross* output, firms bought "unnecessarily large amounts of parts from other firms, receiving credit in [the] final product statistics for things produced by others," while if quotas were measured as *net* output, then firms made as much as possible "even where the cost of parts produced by specialized subcontractors [was] lower" (215).

Selecting a profitable product and resource mix is what entrepreneurs do best, and being productive and alert to better ways of doing their jobs is what employees can do best. It is this specialization and cooperation that gives entrepreneurial companies a competitive edge and enables them to survive and even thrive while other companies are failing. Employees depend on entrepreneurs because their incomes and job security are affected by the quality of business decisions. Alternatively, entrepreneurial success depends to a great extent on the dedication and hard work of a company's employees.

Entrepreneurs also cooperate with their customers. Consumers rely on producers and middle-men to make prudential business decisions so that good products can be purchased at reasonable prices, and entrepreneurs rely on consumer spending to provide the revenue needed to cover their costs and earn a profit. When entrepreneurs cooperate with their employees and customers, all parties are more likely to achieve their ultimate ends. Each person is able to transform possessions and talents into other more preferred things that would otherwise be inaccessible.

KNOWLEDGE REQUIREMENTS IN THE EXTENDED SOCIAL ORDER

"I, Pencil" demonstrates that the extended social order minimizes knowledge requirements for each individual. It has even been suggested that the average self-reliant cave dweller living in the distant past may have required more knowledge just to survive than we need today to live quite comfortably (Sowell 1980, 6–8). In order to survive, primitive people needed to know what wild vegetation they could eat, what water was drinkable, which animals could be hunted with minimal risk, and where they could safely sleep. They also needed to know folk remedies that could be used for serious illnesses that are now easily treatable. Early man had to fabricate footwear, construct clothing, build shelters, and create many other things such as spears, bows, and arrows. If modern man were to find himself alone in this environment he probably wouldn't survive for more than a few days. At the same time, a primitive native in a major city such as Chicago or even in the small town of St. Augustine, Florida, would not likely survive for very long.

Our civilization today is characterized by a tremendous amount of knowledge, and requirements for each occupation can be substantial. The number of years needed to become a psychiatrist, or a mechanical engineer, or a tax attorney exceeds the average life span of prehistoric man. The intellectual advantage that people now have over the primitive savage "is not necessarily that each civilized man has more knowledge but that he *requires* far *less*" (6–8). A contemporary accountant doesn't need to know much more than accounting to live quite well. She drives a very complicated vehicle home that she may only know how to start and drive. She walks into a house knowing nothing about the myriad details involved in its construction. She switches on the lights, uses a can opener, and cooks food in a microwave oven without having to know the mechanical and electrical principles involved in the provision of these items. "Civilization is an enormous device for economizing on knowledge. The time and effort (including costly mistakes) necessary to acquire knowledge are minimized through specialization . . ." (6–8). While the primitive savage must accomplish many varied tasks for himself, and primitive communities must repeatedly duplicate this knowledge through the generations, in the modern society only a "handful of civilized people know how to produce food, a different handful how to produce clothing, medicine, electronics, [and] houses" (6–8). Because knowledge and experience no longer have to be widely duplicated throughout the population, there can be a higher development of knowledge in various specialties that gives entrepreneurs many opportunities to apply unique knowledge to advance their enlightened self-interest and improve the lives of their fellow citizens.

PHYSICAL FALLACY IN THE
EXTENDED SOCIAL ORDER

In the extended order of peaceful social cooperation, economic value is subjective. This means that the same physical object is valued differently, depending on where it is located "in time and space, and according to the risks associated with it. Otherwise people would not go to the trouble and expense of transporting things, or insuring them, or buying them on credit with interest charges" (67). A dominant belief until the late nineteenth century was that objects have the same value regardless of circumstances. This idea, known as the "physical fallacy," has had varying and sometimes pernicious consequences. The labor theory of value, for example, posited that the value of a physical item was intrinsic, and based on the number of labor hours required for the item's production. If digging a hole in the ground and fabricating a chair both take twenty-five hours, then the value of these two things should be the same. Similarly, the value and price of a heavy woolen coat sold in Florida should be the same as in Alaska.

An early manifestation of the "physical fallacy" was the concept of "just price." During the Middle Ages, this idea led to the persecution and prosecution of sellers who dared ask a price that was sinfully at variance with the officially approved price. In addition, the practice of *usury*, or charging interest on loaned money, was considered to be in conflict with Christian theology. During much of the fifteenth century, when the Medici family dominated banking in Italy, usury was considered to be *the* major sin committed by the wealthy. Unlike other sinners, the usurer was destined for hell unless full restitution was paid prior to his death. The reason usury was condemned by the Roman Catholic Church was not because the poor were being taken advantage of since loans were generally made to creditworthy people who had means of repayment. Rather, the Church considered multiplication of money associated with interest as an unnatural form of "copulation." Further, usurers could advance their position in society without human toil, which religious authorities believed was in violation of God's plan for how man should become a fully functioning human being.

For almost one hundred years, five generations of the Medici family wanted to go to heaven, but they also wanted to accumulate wealth from the business of banking and charging interest. They solved this dilemma by inventing acceptable ways of bypassing Church prohibitions. The Church, for example, would regularly borrow money from Medici branch banks as an advance against tributes it expected to receive from all over Europe. The bank's risk of a Church default on these loans was very low because tributes paid to the Church were very dependable. Delayed or missed payments might result in excommunication and, according to belief of the time, a trip straight to hell. Since usury was a sin, the Church would later repay the bank exactly the same amount it had borrowed. Because these banks were also trading companies, to make up for interest income they were forbidden to receive they would sell merchandise to the Church at higher than normal prices.

Another entrepreneurial innovation was stimulated by Church officials who expected some form of compensation for their personal deposit accounts. The Medici banks accomplished this by setting up special confidential deposits to which they added annual payments that were categorized as "gifts." The size of gifts each year would approximate the amount of interest that would have been paid if it had not been sinful to do so. To be considered gifts these sums were supposed to be freely given at the discretion of bankers, which was not always the case. In Florence, for example, at the same time the government was condemning usury it was enacting rules obliging banks to pay promised gifts (Parks 2005, ch. 1).

Even today the "physical fallacy" underlies a lingering bias against middle-men whose primary purpose is not to create new things, but to create value "by relocating them, holding them to times that are more convenient, assuming various risks by stocking inventories" (Sowell 1980, 68). Middle-men create value by using specialized knowledge that is different than the manufacturer's knowledge of production techniques. They also provide low-cost facilities that can be used for storing large quantities of goods purchased directly from the manufacturer, which is something most consumers cannot do. The efficient specialization of middlemen in the extended social order provides convenience and lowers costs for consumers.

It is also because of the "physical fallacy" that individual imagination and creativity may be underestimated. An example is provided by Walt Disney, who experienced early success with a cartoon character named Oswald the Lucky Rabbit. The copyright for this character was held by a movie distributor rather than Disney, and the distributor decided to save the expense of using Disney by hiring away his cartoonists. Disney's contribution was not considered important since he did not actually draw the cartoon and was not involved in the production and marketing of the stories. What was overlooked by the distributor was the value of Disney's imagination and his ability to create compelling fantasies. Without Disney's ideas, Oswald Rabbit soon became a box office flop. The distributor discovered that "The physical things—the drawings, the film, and the theaters—were merely vehicles" for Disney's creativity (71). It wasn't long before Disney created and copyrighted the character Mickey Mouse, which became a new vehicle for his imagination. This example demonstrates how entrepreneurs sometimes make highly valuable contributions that transcend the physical things required to successfully operate a business.

ECONOMIC AND POLITICAL FREEDOM

The extended market order characterized by individuals making personal decisions using their private means is an anomaly in a world where the norm has been powerful authorities who command individuals to adhere to their political and economic schemes. As observed by John Williams: "Monarchs knew what was best for their subjects and told them what to do. Feudal lords knew what was best for their serfs and directed their activities. Aristocrats knew what was best for the masses and dictated how these lesser mortals should spend their days" (27).

In their rejection of the authoritarian norm, America's Founders considered the protection of property to be an essential part of their *Novus Ordo Seclorum* (new order of the ages). James Madison observed that *property* is typically defined as "that dominion which one man claims and exercises over the external things of the world, in exclusion of every other individual" (Madison 1792/1865, 478). He went on to suggest that property has a "larger and juster meaning." Correctly understood, property "embraces everything to which a man may attach a value and have a right, and *which leaves to every one else the like advantage*" (479). In this broader sense, an individual has a property in his "opinions, and the free communication of them . . . in the safety and liberty of his person . . . [and] in the free use of his faculties, and free choice of the objects on which to employ them" (480). For Madison, "as a man is said to have a right to his property, he may be equally said to have a property in his rights," and a just government protects "property of every sort" (480). "To guard a man's house as his castle" is admirable, but this gives a political authority "no title to invade a man's conscience, which is more sacred than his castle" (479).

Some people, who want to replace the extended social order with a centrally planned and directed economy, have suggested that a political authority can protect nonmaterial rights without also protecting "the external things of the world." Evidence collected by Nobel laureate Milton Friedman does not support this idea. In his study of multiple countries over long periods of time, Friedman found that all countries experiencing political freedom also had a considerable amount of economic freedom.

Friedman used freedom of speech as an example to explain his findings. Freedom of speech is a right that should enable individuals, if they so choose, to advocate a peaceful overthrow of the existing government. To finance such a cause requires earning a living so that resources can be pooled "to hold public meetings, publish pamphlets, buy radio time, issue newspapers and magazines, and so on" (Friedman 1962/1982, 17). In a society with economic freedom, this income flows from successful entrepreneurs who pay their employees for their services. In complete absence of economic freedom, individuals work for the state at jobs assigned by the state, and they receive payment from the state at levels determined by the state. It is hard to imagine that the state would turn a blind eye to those employees who are propagandizing the state's overthrow. Work assignments and incomes of dissidents would surely be adversely affected. Leon Trotsky, Russian Marxist revolutionary and founder of the Red Army, wrote: "In a country where the sole employer is the State, opposition means death by slow starvation. The old principle: who does not work shall not eat, has been replaced by a new one: who does not obey shall not eat" (Trotsky 1937, 283). It's also hard to imagine that the most prosperous officials who occupy the highest political positions and the state-run banks would have an interest in financing a call for radical change.

Moreover, even if funding were to become available, the state owns and controls the internet, the meeting halls, the radio and television stations, the newspapers and magazines, and the factories and other resources required by the various modes of communication. It is unlikely that a government would make these media available to the radicals. Alternatively, in a society with economic freedom dissidents only have to convince a few wealthy individuals to support their ideas. Friedrich Engels, for example, the eldest son of a wealthy manufacturer of cotton, provided economic support for Karl Marx that enabled him to write *Das Kapital*. Even without a wealthy patron, all a dissenter must do is convince the manager of a business that propagating an idea "can be financially successful; that the newspaper or magazine or book or other venture will be profitable. The competitive publisher . . . cannot afford to publish only writing with which he personally agrees" (Friedman 1962, 17–18).

During Senator Joseph McCarthy's early 1950s witch hunt for communists working in the US State Department, many individuals were forced to find alternative employment outside of government. A large proportion of these outcasts "went into the most competitive sectors of the economy . . . No one who buys bread knows whether the wheat from which it is made was grown by a Communist or a Republican, by a constitutionalist or a Fascist" (21). It is "one of the great merits of a free society that material reward is *not* dependent on whether the majority of our fellows like or esteem us personally" (Hayek 1996, 54). In the extended social order, honorable entrepreneurs do not have to cower before intimidating political authorities who can withhold material rewards for not following production quota orders. "It is the essence of a free society that we should be materially rewarded not for doing what others order us to do, but for giving them what they want" (54).

With freedom comes responsibility, and there is no guarantee that free people will not develop habits and beliefs inimical to institutions required for their economic and political freedoms. The extended social order that is required for political freedom works best when moral and honorable people are pursuing their enlightened self-interest. Edmund Burke observed:

> Men are qualified for civil liberty, in exact proportion to their disposition to put moral chains upon their own appetites . . . Society cannot exist unless a controlling power upon will and appetite be placed somewhere, and the less of it there is within, the more of it there must be without (Burke 1771).

Liberty and moral virtue are mutually supportive; moral virtue depends upon the freedom of individuals to make the right choices, and liberty depends on moral virtue. In Burke's words: "it is ordained in the eternal constitution of things, that men of intemperate minds cannot be free. Their passions forge their fetters" (Burke 1771).

THE EXTENDED ORDER AND INTERVENTIONISM

Prudence is an important virtue for entrepreneurs pursuing their private interests in the extended social order. To make goods and services affordable while earning a profit, entrepreneurs undertake projects that they anticipate will meet the most urgent needs of buyers, and they continually search for efficient ways to accomplish this task. If successful, they are rewarded by revenues that exceed costs. Alternatively, they are punished by losses if there are unforeseen changes in circumstances detrimental to their projects or if they misjudge buyers' preferences or are unable to find cost-effective means of production and distribution.

A political authority that intervenes in the extended social order can command, forbid, tax, and subsidize for the purpose of forcing or inducing entrepreneurs to change how they allocate resources. Justification for such actions is varied and may include a belief that the "authority is wiser than its subjects with their limited intelligence," or that "it knows better what furthers the happiness of the individual than he himself pretends to know," or that it "feels called upon to sacrifice the welfare of the individual to the well-being of the whole" (Mises 1940/2011, 12).

When a political solution is conceived to solve a problem of the hour, the virtue of prudence is sometimes not high on the authority's list of priorities. Trade-offs, comparing time-adjusted benefits and costs, may be ignored by politicians who claim that using such a formal analysis neglects many benefits not measurable using standard economic calculus. Demonstrating the aphorism that perfect is the enemy of good, grand projects requiring significant funding may be undertaken to solve big problems "once and for all," and if desired results are not produced, then determined politicians will request more funding to achieve a final and complete solution. This can impose a burden on citizens for decades in the form of taxes *and* higher prices. Referred to by Adam Smith as the "man of system," such a political problem solver "is apt to be very wise in his own conceit; and is often so enamored with the supposed beauty of his own ideal plan of government, that he cannot suffer the smallest deviation from any part of it" (Smith 1759/1982, 233–34). Instead of admitting that a partial solution to the problem may be possible if modifications are made to his ideal plan, the "man of system" will continue his quixotic pursuit. Such a person, in Smith's words, will establish the plan: "completely and in all its parts, without any regard either to the great interests, or to the strong prejudices which may oppose it. He seems to imagine that he can arrange the different members of a great society with as much ease as the hand arranges the different pieces upon a chess-board" (233–34).

Consider three examples of interventionist policies that have not seemed to be characterized by the virtue of prudence. In the first example, a panel of British and French "experts" conducted an "objective analysis" to determine an industry that would be a catalyst for stimulating economic growth and employment. Once identified, steps were taken in the 1970s by British and French governments to collaborate and create what they believed would be a technological breakthrough. And so they developed a supersonic plane that could fly from New York to London in half the time it took standard jets to make the trip (Roberts 2007, 65–67).

The planning authority apparently didn't foresee that this innovation would not meet the most urgent needs of buyers. Perhaps the market for this service was small because the $10,000 fare in 1999 was seven times higher than for a normal jet. This project was a financial disaster for investors, and British and French taxpayers. By 1976, when the Concorde first flew, $4.3 billion had already been invested. Seven years later revenues barely covered operating costs and the entire initial investment was written off. The Concorde was finally grounded in 2003 and can now only be found in museums. During its short life the Concorde project provided a subsidy to rich travelers that was mostly paid for by middle-income British and French taxpayers. In addition, no technological spillover benefits that the planning experts had predicted were generated by this project (65–67). The planners and politicians learned a hard lesson that "in the great chess-board of human society, every single piece has a principle of motion of its own, altogether different from that which the legislature might choose to impress upon it" (Smith, 1759/1982, 234).

A second example of a political solution that has ignored economic trade-offs involves subsidies being provided to the wind energy industry. Politicians and industry proponents argue that subsidies are justified because wind power is "vitally important" for America's "clean energy" future; it will help prevent global warming; and an elimination of wind energy subsidies will destroy many jobs that "states can't afford to lose." The wind energy industry's social and economic costs, which are significant, are rarely discussed. For example, wind turbines require a substantial amount of fossil fuels. During the year they average 30 percent of their rated capacity (compared to more than 90 percent for coal and gas fired plants), and they operate at only 5 percent of rated capacity during the hottest and coldest parts of the year when they are most needed. Excess electricity that they produce during slack demand periods cannot be stored for peak demand periods. Backup generators using hydrocarbons must be constantly run, and electricity is frequently drawn rather than added to the electrical grid to keep the wind blades turning (Driessen 2012).

Another problem is that wind energy is not eco-friendly when taking into account the extraction and use of enormous amounts of rare earth metals and other raw materials required to manufacture, deliver and install the turbines, backup generators and high voltage transmission lines. Wind turbines and transmission lines also require vast amounts of crop, scenic and wildlife habitat land. A 600-megawatt wind installation needs 40,000 to 50,000 acres which is 250 times more than a 600-megawatt coal or gas-fired power plant. In addition, because wind installations must be located where it is windy, which is typically hundreds of miles away from cities, thousands of additional acres for transmission lines is required. An additional environmental cost is that wind turbines annually kill more than half a million eagles, hawks, falcons, vultures, ducks, geese, bats and other rare, threatened, endangered and otherwise protected flying creatures. While oil companies have been prosecuted for the deaths of as few as a dozen birds, turbine operators have been granted a blanket exemption from endangered and migratory species laws and penalties (Driessen 2012).

By 2013, US taxpayers were providing as much as $10 billion in annual subsidies to sustain 37,000 jobs in this industry for an average of $270,000 per wind job. With further growth of this industry the United States will experience lessons already learned by Spain, Germany, Britain, and other countries; wind energy mandates and subsidies drive up the price of electricity in all segments of society, and has caused the loss of at least two traditional jobs for every wind job created (Driessen 2012).

The issue of global warming provides a third example of a political solution that has been immune to a consideration of economic costs. This was clearly demonstrated by a project that was undertaken by the Copenhagen Consensus Center (CCC), which operates as a unit of the Copenhagen Business School. In 2004, CCC, under the direction of Bjørn Lomborg, hosted a group of eight prominent economists, including four Nobel laureates, to establish priorities if $50 billion were to become available to ameliorate ten world crises previously selected for consideration. The process had begun earlier with a CCC review of all major United Nations' publications from 2000 through 2003. A long list of issues addressed in this material was narrowed to thirty-one, and this shortened list was reviewed for completeness by two Danish focus groups, one composed of economists and the other of non-economists. These two groups endorsed the thirty-one issues and added "digital divide" as a topic worthy of consideration. The eight "expert" economists were then asked to whittle down the thirty-two issues to ten challenge areas that they believed offered the best opportunity for improvement. The ten areas selected were climate change, communicable diseases, conflicts and arms proliferation, access to education, financial instability, governance and corruption, malnutrition and hunger, migration, sanitation and access to clean water, and subsidies and trade barriers (Lomborg 2004, 4–5).

Once the challenge areas were identified, CCC commissioned ten economic "specialists," each of whom was highly regarded for research in the area to which he or she was assigned. Each specialist was asked to write a paper to address "dimensions of the challenge" and to identify up to five realistic and politically relevant opportunities for dealing with the challenge. Since the marginal cost of incremental improvements in a challenge area would be expected to increase sharply beyond some point, opportunities were to be framed to offer partial solutions to particular problems. Thus, instead of analyzing an allocation of funds to supply the world with clean drinking water, a realistic opportunity would be to fund the supply of drinkable water to, say, half the world's population who currently do not have it. Specialists were also asked to include a survey of cost-benefit studies and, if possible, to apply this technique to the opportunities they were proposing. Two additional economists in each challenge area were commissioned to write "perspective" papers for the purpose of providing commentary and presenting alternative points of view to ideas in the challenge paper (4). The final step was for the eight experts and ten specialists to meet over a five-day period to discuss the challenges and opportunities that were identified for this project. The eight economists finally met alone to discuss and rank the opportunities. To reduce the incidence of strategic ranking, a final common list of opportunities was constructed using the median of the expert rankings (7–8). The idea of this project was not to pick the world's most significant problems, but to choose opportunities within challenge areas that offered the greatest potential payoff per dollar spent using standard cost-benefit analysis. Thus, access to education, conflicts, and financial instability were left off the final list because of insurmountable difficulties, while other challenges were listed several times because of multiple high-payoff opportunities.

The final list identified the following seventeen opportunities within seven challenge areas: [1] Communicable diseases (Control of HIV/AIDS); [2] Malnutrition and hunger (Providing micronutrients); [3] Subsidies and trade (Trade liberalization); [4] Communicable diseases (Control of malaria); [5] Malnutrition and hunger (Development of new agricultural technologies); [6] Sanitation and water (Community-managed water supply and sanitation); [7] Sanitation and water (Small-scale water technology for livelihoods); [8] Sanitation and water (Research on water productivity in food production); [9] Governance and corruption (Lowering the cost of starting a new business); [10] Migration (Lowering barriers to migration for skilled workers); [11] Malnutrition and hunger (improving infant and child nutrition); [12] Communicable diseases (Scaled up basic health services); [13] Malnutrition and hunger (Reducing the prevalence of LBW [i.e., low-birthweight pregnancy]); [14] Migration (Guest worker programs for the unskilled); [15] Climate change (Optimal carbon tax); [16] Climate change (The Kyoto Protocol); and [17] Climate change (Value-at-risk carbon tax) (606). The experts considered the first four items on the list as "Very Good" opportunities for improving the listed challenges. Opportunities were viewed as "Good" for numbers 5–9, "Fair" for numbers 10–13, and "Bad" for numbers 14–17 (608).

The Copenhagen Consensus project was valuable in many respects. It examined world crises with an economist's eye and posed this question: In a world with scarce resources what should be our highest priorities? Importantly, it pointed out the silliness of spending large sums on global warming, which has a projected benefit-cost ratio of less than four using a zero discount rate, and that drops below one when the discount rate is two percent or higher. The benefit-cost ratio for the top-ranked HIV/AIDS opportunity was estimated to be 49.9 using a three percent discount rate (37 and 104).

If interventionist policy solutions are "undertaken in full recognition of their effects, if the authority is fully aware of what it is doing and what results it will accomplish, one might disapprove of its action only if one does not approve of its aim" (Mises 1940/2011, 20). However, if political solutions are instituted without taking into account associated costs, then interventionism diverts resources from more efficient uses, diminishes aggregate wealth creation, and reduces quality of life. Unreflective interventionism violates general rules of property and eviscerates the significant benefits created by entrepreneurs guided by prospective profits.

SUMMARY AND CONCLUSIONS

Honorable entrepreneurs who live their lives exercising superior prudence can balance a pursuit of overlapping material and nonmaterial ends, achieve both material success *and* happiness, and advance the public good. Such entrepreneurs are the lifeblood of an extended social order as they serve others by creating new forms of business, improving ways of relocating things in time and space, and unlocking and transforming the world's hidden resources. By continually shifting resources from lower to higher areas of productivity and value, they solve social crises and create wealth that is widespread throughout society. Their self-interest includes the interests of researchers who discover cures for virulent diseases; the interests of philanthropists who spend their previously accumulated riches helping people in need; and the interests of producers who enrich themselves by making goods more affordable for the poor.

As seen in "I, Pencil," entrepreneurs extend the market's scope by coordinating the use of widely "dispersed bits of incomplete and frequently contradictory knowledge," which no single person can possibly have possession of (Hayek 1945, 519). By being alert to opportunity and adapting to circumstances revealed by continually changing product and resource prices, entrepreneurs are primary actors in a peaceful social order praised thusly by F. A. Hayek:

> I am convinced that if it were the result of deliberate human design, and if the people guided by the price changes understood that their decisions have significance far beyond their immediate aim, this mechanism would have been acclaimed as one of the greatest triumphs of the human mind (527).

In the search for better ways of creating value, entrepreneurs have generally flourished when they have been free to pursue private ends using their own means. In Johnson's fable and around the world today, when freedom and personal enterprise are limited, opportunities for self-improvement are diminished, hopes for living a *choice of life* are dashed, and the ability to serve others is sharply curtailed. While freedom enables entrepreneurs to pursue material success and happiness, there is no guarantee that either of these ends will be attained. Accepting the risk of being compensated for how well other members of society are served creates the possibility of significant loss even when working long hours with exceptional skill and knowledge. What freedom provides is a chance for entrepreneurs to take risks if they choose, live their lives to the fullest, pursue happiness as they perceive it, develop a business they have dreamed of, and create the kind of person they want to be.

Chapter Three

Virtues and Honor in the *Practice* of Entrepreneurship

More than a few social theorists and editorial writers portray entrepreneurs as coldhearted decision-makers who are motivated solely by material gain. They contend that entrepreneurs are selfish and greedy, and they declare that everyone would be better off if businesses would abandon the pursuit of profit. More than a few politicians have built their public careers on condemnation of entrepreneurial success, which they claim is achieved on the backs of customers and employees.

This does not accurately portray the work of honorable entrepreneurs. Entrepreneurs who are honorable achieve long-term success by cooperating with their customers and employees in ways that create widespread benefit. Uncoerced transactions foster a social alchemy that enables all participants to transform their talents and possessions into other more preferred things and to achieve ends that would otherwise be impossible by working alone.

Honorable entrepreneurs have a keen sense of community and are guided by religious and ethical beliefs, customs and traditions, and aesthetic value judgments. All are self-loving to some degree, which is characteristic of most human beings, but they are also self-judging. In an extended social order where most buyers and sellers are not personally known, profit is the means by which buyers reveal their preferences to sellers. Profit is a reward entrepreneurs earn for efficiently meeting the strongest felt needs and preferences of consumers. It is *the* critical link that ties together diverse interests across multiple product and resource markets.

Chapter 3

VIRTUES AND HONOR OF AN ENTREPRENEUR

For Aristotle, all human action is aimed at achieving some good that is perceived differently by different people at the same time, and differently by the same people at different times depending on circumstances. When a person is sick he may imagine that health is the ultimate good, while if he is poor and in good health he may believe that wealth is the primary good. Wealth and pleasure, which are commonly viewed as final goods worthy of pursuit, are actually different ways, sometimes unsuccessful, of achieving the ultimate end in human life, which is happiness (Aristotle c. 340 BC/1973, bk. 1, ch. 4–7).

Aristotle viewed the moral virtues as a mean between excess and deficiency. Courage lies between rashness and cowardice, temperance rests between self-indulgence and insensibility, liberality is the mean between prodigality and meanness, and justice is bounded by doing injustice on the one side and suffering injustice on the other (bk. II, ch. 6–8). Because circumstances determine when a particular action is excessive, deficient or correct, practical wisdom is required to act correctly at the correct time and in the right place. Thus, judgment is an intellectual virtue necessary for exercising the virtues of character (bk. VI, ch. 12). Living a good life entails understanding and achieving excellence in the practice of virtues associated with a desired end.

Enjoyment can be realized when excellence is achieved in any number of activities such as playing chess, composing a play, or creating an architectural rendering of a complex building. In an extended social order, that existed in ancient Athens but was not understood by Aristotle (Hayek 1988, 45–46), it can also be the work of a producer, trader, or creator of a new business. Excellence in any area is determined by evolved standards generally accepted by people actively engaged in that activity. How excellence is achieved and the kind of enjoyment that is experienced depends on a person's judgments about actions that are appropriate as well as what kind of person he or she wants to be. For example, excellence in playing chess requires a study of multiple openings, an understanding of the nuances of complex middle game strategies, and a memorization and mechanical precision of play in the endgame. Similarly, excellence in launching, operating, and liquidating a business involves discernment of the most strongly felt needs of customers, understanding management techniques that can be applied to efficiently operate and grow a business, quick adaptation to unforeseen changes in product and resource markets, and knowledge of when and how to exit a business to harvest the fruits of ownership. If winning is all that matters in chess or other contests, some players may choose to cheat if they can get away with it. Similarly, if profit is all that matters for entrepreneurs, then some will not hesitate to do anything inside and outside the law to achieve their ends.

Alexis de Tocqueville observed that for a social group to improve its standing in society it is in the group's best interest to praise and encourage those practices of members who strengthen the group and to condemn behavior that weakens or undermines the group. Using honor and dishonor to allocate praise and blame respectively, is one way to accomplish this (Tocqueville 1840/1976, 626). Entrepreneurs as a group flourish when their property rights are secure, and they are free to compete in an extended social order. The "prerequisite for the existence of property, freedom, and order, from the time of the Greeks to the present" has been the same: "law in the sense of abstract rules" (Hayek 1988, 30). Entrepreneurs are honorable, in the sense of Tocqueville, when they adhere to general rules of property and just conduct and avoid actions that are personally advantageous but detrimental to the extended social order. Their reflections of how actions affect the extended social order are "motives of rational action, provided people think them significant" and are just as important "as those normally called economic" (Mises 1936/1981, 99–100). While honorable entrepreneurs are only making provisional sacrifices that will yield greater benefits in the long-run, their just conduct is praiseworthy because they must sometimes endure greater risk and realize less material success than the violators of general rules. Principled entrepreneurs who hold themselves to a higher standard are betrayed by dishonorable crony competitors who benefit from preferential treatment provided by their political sponsors.

Aristotle's view of honor was that individuals of superior refinement consider it to be the highest final good. Honor, however, does not consistently produce happiness because criteria for this distinction can be twisted so that it is withheld or taken away from a deserving person. It is because of this that Aristotle regarded the cultivation of virtue as a superior means of achieving happiness (Aristotle c. 340 BC/1973, bk. 1, ch. 5). If Aristotelian virtue is defined as "*an acquired human quality the possession and exercise of which tends to enable us to achieve those goods which are internal to practices*" (MacIntyre 1981/2007, 191), then the virtue of just conduct in the *practice* of entrepreneurship entails achieving excellence using *economic means* to acquire external goods of material success, while knowing and exercising those internal qualities that strengthen and preserve the institutions upon which the extended social order depends.

In addition to the virtue of just conduct, internal goods of honorable entrepreneurs are the intellectual virtues of insight, imagination and practical wisdom, and the moral virtues of courage, prudence, truth, and liberality. Achieving the external good of profit in an extended social order requires entrepreneurial excellence in a continual search for better and more efficient ways of satisfying unmet needs of consumers. Economist Israel Kirzner has identified standards of entrepreneurial excellence that can produce profit, while increasing a community's wealth through provision of better products, and transformation of resources in new and useful ways. Astute entrepreneurs are "calculating agents" who are "alert to opportunities" that are "just around the corner" and "that may turn up." They recognize opportunities that others don't see because they know "when to obtain information and how to deploy it" (Kirzner 1979, 7–8). In his comparison of someone who has imagination and someone who does not, Baron de Montesquieu observed that they "see things as differently as two fictional heroes, one of whom is captivated by what he sees and the other not." While the first sees "crystal walls, ruby roofs, silver streams, diamond tables," the other "perceives only hideous rocks and an arid countryside" (Montesquieu 1748/1977, 438).

Business management professionals read popular books promoting particular techniques that are presented as new methods of ensuring company success, and examples of successful firms employing these methods are used to demonstrate the efficacy of the books' recommendations. It's not uncommon to find these same companies a few years later experiencing problems unforeseen by the books' authors. The earlier books will then be replaced by new books once again making claims about newly perceived ideas that are guaranteed to work. While ordinary business executives "read the book" of the hour, an entrepreneur who possesses imagination is more likely to use practical wisdom to "write the book," at least in his or her own mind. Each story is characterized by a strong desire to overcome what may seem to be an insoluble problem or an unmet need. One story may be about how to solve a financial crisis that occurs unexpectedly because a creditor doesn't honor his obligation, while another may address how to more efficiently remove seeds from cotton fibers. The most successful entrepreneurs write and rewrite their own books as they navigate their businesses through waters that are sometimes turbulent in hopes of discovering better ways of satisfying their customers. They constantly evaluate their businesses and themselves with an eye on continual improvement, and their acute awareness of opportunity is expressed by a Shakespearean metaphor:

> There is a tide in the affairs of men, / Which, taken at the flood, leads on to fortune; / Omitted, all the voyage of their life / Is bound in shallows, and in miseries (Shakespeare 1623/1998, *Julius Caesar*, act 4, scene 3).

Aristotelian virtue in the *practice* of entrepreneurship fosters social cohesion and general human flourishing. The importance of just conduct was emphasized by Adam Smith when he wrote that the "prevalence of injustice must utterly destroy" a society:

Justice . . . is the main pillar that upholds the whole edifice. If it is removed, the great, the immense fabric of human society, the fabric which to raise and support seems in this world, if I may say so, to have been the peculiar and darling care of Nature, must in a moment crumble into atoms (Smith 1759/1982, 86).

Although the roads to material success and to virtue are the same for honorable entrepreneurs, many successful people achieve their ends through "flattery and falsehood" rather than "merit and abilities" (63). Honorable entrepreneurs may or may not achieve their hoped-for external goods, but they always apply practical wisdom to cultivate their internal goods in the pursuit of material ends. The internal good of just conduct and external good of honor cannot be realized by those in business who may be technically astute in their management decisions but don't adhere to standards necessary for perpetuation of the extended order of peaceful social cooperation.

There are three categories of entrepreneurs that diminish the extended order's social alchemy. First, there are those who are ignorant about how their actions can adversely affect this order. They generally adhere to the Rule of Law but periodically seek and sometimes benefit from preferential legislation in violation of general rules. Second, there are entrepreneurs who understand that their actions, while legal, are injurious to the long-run public good. Their failing is not ignorance concerning the consequences of their decisions but is rather a lack of willpower to resist short-run advantages that can be gained by violating general rules of property and just conduct. Third, there are unscrupulous CEOs who willingly violate the law to achieve their ends.

Entrepreneurs belonging to the first group lack the intellectual virtue to be honorable but they are not dishonorable. Actions of honorable entrepreneurs have moral weight because justification of choices is understood and decisions are consistently informed by this knowledge. Because of their ignorance, bad choices gradually replace good habits that are uninformed by principle and vulnerable to the vagaries of time and the "slings and arrows of outrageous fortune." Members of the dishonorable second, and immoral third groups pose a greater immediate threat to the vitality of American social life.

While critics' claims of business exploitation are bolstered by activities of the criminal third group, it should be noted that actions of con artists who defraud people, executives who engage in deceptive accounting practices, and managers who obstruct justice are not unique to the economic system. In business, politics, and all other segments of society, there are always individuals willing to advance their interests at the expense of others. Russian theologian Aleksandr Solzhenitsyn observed that "the line dividing good and evil cuts through the heart of every human being," and this bifurcation is intractable because no one "is willing to destroy a piece of his own heart" (Solzhenitsyn 1973/1985, 75). So while some bad people are engaged in business, it is not business that has made them bad. "The economic relation, or business nexus," wrote Philip Wicksteed, "is necessary alike for carrying on the life of the peasant and the prince, of the saint and the sinner . . . of the most altruistic and the most egoistic of men" (Wicksteed 1910, bk. 1, ch. 5). Fortunately, it is only a handful of business knaves who take questionable shortcuts or commit outright acts of fraud to enhance their incomes at the expense of their employees, customers, lenders, and stockholders. Unfortunately, periodic business scandals spawned by these individuals give all entrepreneurs a bad name and can inflict great damage on their companies and society at large.

THE BUSINESS NARCISSUS

The dishonest entrepreneur whose excessive self-love wrecks his company and the personal lives of those who depend on him is a modern-day Narcissus. In the Greek myth, Narcissus's mother learns from a seer that her child will live a full life only by restraining his egoism. He is unable to do this, and through his early years Narcissus takes pleasure in teasing and then destroying his many admirers who are mesmerized by his outward appearance. Narcissus's cruel rejection of the nymph Echo, who is one of his most ardent fans, causes her to experience extraordinary grief. She begins living in caves and mountain cliffs, and because of extreme loneliness she fades away and becomes invisible. Nothing is left of Echo but her voice that can only repeat what others have said.

One day following a long hunt a thirsty Narcissus discovers a clear spring, and while leaning over to quench his thirst he falls in love with the stunning image he sees in the water. Narcissus tries to embrace the beautiful boy and is frustrated when he discovers it is his own reflection. Day after day Narcissus gazes into the pool of water aching to possess what he sees, while knowing that it is not possible. Narcissus is shattered by the grief of not being able to have the one thing in the world he wants most. And so, with a sympathetic Echo looking on, Narcissus ends his life with a dagger.

Economists instruct aspiring entrepreneurs that the only way to achieve long-run success is to win a daily market election with consumers casting their dollar votes. "Each ballot of the consumers," wrote Ludwig von Mises, "adds only a little to the elected man's sphere of action. To reach the upper levels of entrepreneurship he needs a great number of votes, repeated again and again over a long period of time, a protracted series of successful strokes. He must stand every day a new trial, must submit anew to reelection as it were" (Mises 1952/2008, 147).

The impatient business Narcissus values success above everything else, and he pursues fame and fortune using unsavory means such as accounting sleights of hand that hide losses or that make his company's profits seem more robust than they actually are. He does this with little regard for employees, stockholders, and lenders. The outward appearance of the business Narcissus attracts commercial suitors who desperately want to be a part of this success. Images of the business Narcissus appear on the covers of prominent magazines that extol his ingenuity and business prowess. Careless auditors and investment analysts echo the business Narcissus's claims of monumental success.

At the turn of the century the Enron Narcissus said, "We are very profitable," and the Arthur Anderson Echo repeated, "Very profitable," and when Enron Narcissus proclaimed, "You should invest heavily in the company," investment advisors echoed "Invest heavily in the company." In the end, the self-admiring business Narcissus stared into a pool of debt while trying to preserve an image of success, and when the inevitable failure came, Enron Narcissus and Arthur Anderson Echo pointed fingers at each other. Narcissus exclaimed, "We did nothing wrong," and Echo repeated "We did nothing wrong," and when Narcissus said, "It is their fault," Echo repeated, "It is their fault." When this Houston, Texas–based energy company finally self-destructed and its auditor was dissolved, lenders, stockholders and employees had lost billions of dollars. At the very end:

> Narcissus' tears defac'd the surface of the well, with circle after circle, as they fell: . . . Echo saw him in his present misery . . . "Farewel," says he; the parting sound scarce fell from his faint lips, but Echo reply'd, "farewel." Then on th' wholsome earth he gasping lyes, till death shuts up those self-admiring eyes (Ovid 8 AD/1885, 212).

CRONY CAPITALISM'S IGNOBLE DECEPTION

In Plato's dialogue, *The Republic*, Socrates argues that while truth is valuable and should be generally revered (Plato c. 380–360 BC/1985, 85, 389b), a case can be made for a lie perpetrated by a city-state's rulers if this strengthens the philosopher king's ability to effect a good and just society. A political authority that carefully foments such a deception can create benefits for citizens in much the same way that a doctor can improve their health by prescribing medicine (389b). A noble lie can strengthen the resolve of warriors who are charged with guarding the city and keeping the peace, and can deepen citizen loyalty to the Republic's first principles (112–13, 414b–c).

A noble lie must be convincingly articulated to produce its intended effects. In an earlier dialogue, *Menexenus*, Socrates mockingly describes how he is only temporarily affected by the words of disingenuous rhetoricians:

[I]n every conceivable form they praise the city; and they praise those who died in war, and all our ancestors who went before us; and they praise ourselves also who are still alive, until I feel quite elevated by their laudations . . . This consciousness of dignity lasts me more than three days, and not until the fourth or fifth day do I come to my senses and know where I am (Plato c. 387–380 BC/1892, 775–76, 235).

In a more serious vein, David Hume pinpoints why oratory can be extremely important for the durability of a governmental authority:

Nothing appears more surprising to those, who consider human affairs with a philosophical eye, than the easiness with which the many are governed by the few; and the implicit submission, with which men resign their own sentiments and passions to those of their rulers. When we enquire by what means this wonder is effected, we shall find, that, as FORCE is always on the side of the governed, the governors have nothing to support them but opinion. It is therefore, on opinion only that government is founded; and this maxim extends to the most despotic and the most military governments, as well as to the most free and most popular (Hume 1742/1987a, 32).

While it's debatable whether or not there can be justification for Plato's noble lie today, citizens should never be deceived if the effect of rhetoric is to undermine a political society's ideals (Plato c. 380–360 BC/1985, 85, 389b). This is why deceptions, commonly used by crony capitalists to achieve preferential advantage using *political means*, are ignoble. In addition to sacrificing the material well-being of consumers, taxpayers, and nonpreferred competitors, the dishonorable entrepreneur's partial truths and outright lies damage the public good by diminishing respect for the extended order's general rules of property and justice. *Political means*, justified by ignoble deceptions, are used to acquire many types of preferential legislation, including bailouts, subsidies, favored tax treatment and price fixing, as well as regulation that diminishes the profitability and growth of competitors and that makes it more difficult for new firms to enter a market.

Consider several examples of how crony capitalists use ignoble deceptions and base rhetoric to benefit from bailouts, subsidies, and preferential tax treatment. Following the peak of the financial crisis in 2008, taxpayers funded bailouts of several automobile and financial service companies. General Motors received $50 billion, while $182 billion was spent to save the giant insurance company AIG. The ignoble deception used to justify AIG's bailout was the claim that its failure posed a "systemic risk" to the US economy. It was suggested that if AIG failed, then many other companies important to the economy would also be pulled down and this would cause a collapse of the entire financial sector. Notwithstanding this claim, several bank presidents in congressional testimony said that in the absence of other factors, an AIG failure would not have created problems for their firms. This view was corroborated by IAIS, the international body of insurance regulators (Bennetts 2013).

The Dodd–Frank Wall Street Reform and Consumer Protection Act was passed in 2010 to reduce the systemic risk of large financial market companies such as AIG that are "too big to fail" (TBTF). Unfortunately, Dodd-Frank has made it worse by creating significant competitive advantages for AIG and other enormous financial institutions, enabling them to become even larger. Dodd-Frank illustrates an insight of Nobel laureate economist George Stigler, "that, as a rule, regulation is acquired by the industry and is designed and operated primarily for its benefit" (Stigler 1971, 3). This "reform" empowered the Treasury to unilaterally declare just about any company in the financial sector TBTF so that taxpayers can now become responsible for future bailouts of insurance companies, hedge funds, private equity companies, and investment advisers to name a few. This creates a "moral hazard" problem because executives of large companies, in anticipation that their firms will qualify for TBTF designation, have an incentive to make risky decisions and hold riskier assets. They know that customers of TBTF firms need not worry about loss of premiums or coverage, and shareholders do not fear bankruptcy. Further, crony capitalists running companies that are already designated TBTF have a competitive advantage in that the Federal Reserve must "stringently" regulate these companies. An average customer will believe that a company being closely watched by the Fed has no chance of failure and is necessarily superior to a company that has not been designated TBTF. This means that an AIG will sell more insurance than a competitor, even if this firm is run more prudently and efficiently.

It is telling that large financial institutions, which have supposedly found Dodd-Frank to be onerous, lined up in opposition to proposed reforms being discussed in late 2016. Reform was opposed by executives of J. P. Morgan and Goldman Sachs, and by the presidents of four trade associations representing banks and credit unions (*Wall Street Journal* 2016). One reason for this is that Dodd-Frank drove many smaller financial institutions out of the market because they could not afford to incur the high cost associated with this legislation's requirements, and these smaller firms were easy targets for acquisition by larger financial institutions. In addition, Dodd-Frank continues to impede competition by imposing a significant burden on new firms trying to enter the market.

Consider how crony capitalists in agriculture use ignoble deceptions to obtain subsidies that increase their profitability. Begun in the 1930s to help struggling family farms, subsidy programs have been transformed into a mechanism for benefiting large corporate interests. Since the 1930s the number of farms has declined by 70 percent and only 2 percent of Americans are now directly involved in farming. From 1995 to 2012 farmers received $292.2 billion in subsidies from the Federal government, and "aid" was given even when profits were high. In 2011, the average income of farm households was \$87,289, which was 25.3 percent higher than the average US household income (USDA 2013). One of the most heavily subsidized crops was corn despite the fact that corn prices and profits increased dramatically due to its use in ethanol production.

While the ignoble deception justifying a continuance of farm subsidies is that they are primarily for the benefit of small family farmers, the truth is that owners of large corporate farms reap most of the benefits. Around 62 percent of farms, mostly small, collected no subsidies, while 10 percent of farms, mostly large corporate entities, were paid 75 percent of all subsidies (EWG). The restrictions on agricultural subsidies are so loose that nonfarmers who build houses on land previously used for farming can receive direct payments from the government. Subdivision developers sometimes advertise this benefit to make their properties more saleable.

Two ignoble deceptions in agriculture justify the subsidy of ethanol production, which requires a large quantity of corn. The Renewable Fuels Standard (RFS), which is part of the US alternative energy policy, mandated that 13.6 billion gallons of ethanol be blended into the gasoline supply during 2013, and that this number be increased to 36 billion gallons by 2022. Because corn is the primary source of ethanol, more of this crop is now devoted to fuel than is consumed by livestock. In 2011, 40 percent of the corn produced was blended with gasoline. This has caused high and volatile food prices, which is a problem both at home and abroad, especially in developing countries. When high temperatures and a lack of rainfall reduce the supply of corn, prices spike upward worldwide and citizens of the poorest countries go hungry. A number of peer-reviewed studies have concluded that biofuel mandates increase hunger-related diseases and cause tens of thousands of deaths each year. In recognition of this, a consensus report was requested in 2010 by G-20 countries to address how best to manage risks of food price volatility linked to riots in dozens of countries. Most major global bureaucracies, including the International Monetary Fund, the World Trade Organization, and the World Bank, supported Recommendation Six of the consensus report to "Remove provisions of current national policies that subsidize (or mandate) biofuels production or consumption." Yielding to America's corporate farm and agribusiness crony capitalists, this recommendation has been all but ignored by the Environmental Protection Agency and other US political authorities who have the power to change current policy.

The ignoble deceptions promulgated by corn growers and ethanol processors in support of continuing RFS are that ethanol will help us achieve energy independence, and that ethanol is good for the environment because it reduces the use of carbon-based fuels. Contrary to the first claim, it has been estimated that using the entire corn crop for ethanol would only reduce US oil consumption by 4 percent. The second claim is also deceptive because large amounts of carbon-based fuels are required to fertilize, cultivate, and harvest corn, and still more is required to process and truck the ethanol to refineries. This is why major environmental groups, such as the National Wildlife Federation and Friends of the Earth, now oppose the use of ethanol in gasoline.

Sport stadium deals are another example of subsidies that benefit crony capitalists at the expense of the public good and are justified through the use of an ignoble deception. It is common that more than half of a new stadium's cost is covered by state and local authorities and paid for by raising taxes. The ignoble deception offered in support of these arrangements is that large positive economic benefits will be created in the form of high gameday spending at local establishments; jobs created for constructing the stadium; higher property values; and more robust growth and tax revenue. The evidence is that such deals do not create net positive benefits. A thorough study of sports franchises in thirty-seven cities between 1969 and 1996 found that they had virtually no effect on per-capita income in a city (Shapiro 2012). An older study that looked at twelve stadium areas, from 1958 to 1987, concluded that professional sports was not the primary factor influencing economic growth. A shorter study of forty-six cities, from 1990 to 1994, found that job growth was lower in cities with major league teams. Stanford economist Roger Noll has pointed out that because the majority of fans attending a game live within a twenty-mile radius, money they spend on the sporting event would have likely been spent on other forms of local recreation and entertainment (Shapiro 2012). In some cases, taxpayers have had to continue servicing debt on stadiums long after they have been demolished. In 2013, New Jersey still owed more than $100 million on the old Meadowlands stadium, and King County in Seattle still had to pay $80 million for a Kingdome that no longer existed. While taxpayers foot most of the bill and take most of the risk for constructing new stadiums, "55% of the gains from subsidies to pro sports teams go to players and 45% to owners" (Shapiro 2012).

Preferential tax breaks are another source of income and wealth for crony capitalists. At the beginning of 2013, Democrats and Republicans agreed on a fiscal cliff deal that saw taxes go up for all "millionaires and billionaires" unless they were fortunate enough to own a NASCAR track in Michigan, a wind energy company, a rum distillery, a business located on an Indian reservation, or a tuna company operating in American Samoa. In addition, thanks to the lobbying efforts of former Senator Dodd, crony Hollywood capitalists obtained $430 million in tax breaks for fiscal years 2013 and 2014. Film and television producers were able to "expense the first $15 million of production costs incurred in the United States ($20 million if the costs are incurred in economically depressed areas)" (*Wall Street Journal* 2013). Justification for these tax breaks was the ignoble deception that local economies, where movies are shot, would realize significant and long-term economic benefits. Thus, a movie shot at a remote location in West Virginia earned an additional tax break for Hollywood cronies even though unemployed locals were never hired to fill Hollywood's unionized jobs. Any local stimulus created by this legislation has been short-term and limited. Six Republicans joined thirteen Democrats on the Senate Finance Committee to pass this special "tax extenders" bill that made available $40 billion in benefits to their crony friends.

Other *political means* used by crony capitalists to shield their firms from competition and to earn windfall profits include import quotas and tariffs, and domestic price supports. Import quotas and tariffs currently apply to a wide array of products such as brooms, ethyl alcohol, cotton, wheat gluten, and an assortment of dairy and textile products. Sugar beet and sugar cane producers and processors rely on import quotas, domestic price supports, and an arrangement by which special governmental loans can be secured with sugar that companies have not yet produced. Loans amounting to $862 million in 2013 were secured with 4.1 billion pounds of sugar. In addition to acquiring sugar forfeited by companies that don't repay loans, the United States Department of Agriculture (USDA 2013) planned to buy as much as 400 million pounds to support sugar prices. On top of everything else, sugar acquired by the USDA through loan defaults is sold by the government to ethanol producers at a loss of ten cents per pound (Wexler 2013).

For over thirty years beginning in 1982, Americans had to pay, on average, twice the world price for sugar (28.4 cents compared to 14 cents per pound). The crony sugar capitalists' ignoble deception is that saving sugar jobs is worth the cost. The whole truth of the matter reveals a different story. Taking into account higher prices that must be paid by consumers, and food processing and candy businesses that use sugar inputs, it is estimated that each sugar job that is saved costs approximately $600,000 annually (Pugel 2012, 211). There is also a reduction of other forms of employment because some companies have moved north to Canada to avoid paying high sugar prices, while others remaining in the United States have had to reduce their work force. A 2006 study published by the United States Department of Commerce estimated that for every sugar job saved in the United States, three jobs are lost in the sugar processing industry.

Another preferential policy that benefited crony capitalists at the expense of the public good was President Bush's 2004 tariffs on imported steel that ranged as high as 30 percent. The ignoble deception used by crony steel interests to justify this policy was that eighteen thousand steelworker jobs were saved. What was left unsaid is that the number of jobs lost in the steel-using industry because of higher steel prices was greater than the total number of people working in the steel industry. The political reality of this tariff was that it benefited companies and workers in swing states that President Bush needed for reelection.

Examples of state and local legislation and regulation that benefit crony capitalists include occupational licensing, nonessential technical and product standards that favor particular firms, and "no-bid" contracts that are given to politically connected businesses. The ignoble deception used to justify occupational licensing is that it always makes sense to protect the public by shielding them from incompetent and untrained practitioners. While it makes sense to license some occupations, in many cases licensing only serves to artificially restrict competition and preserve incomes of people already working in affected markets. More than one thousand occupations now require licenses in the United States. Many stipulate excessive training in relation to occupational tasks, and some require instruction that is unrelated to a job. In Texas, for example, computer repair technicians must obtain a degree in criminal justice or serve a three-year apprenticeship under a licensed private investigator to legally fix computers. Without these credentials technicians face $4,000 in fines, a $10,000 civil penalty, and up to one year in jail. In California, a person who installs spikes along the edge of building roofs to discourage roosting pigeons, must first serve a two-year apprenticeship with a licensed pest-control business and pass a lengthy exam on the proper handling and use of pesticides.

A 2012 report issued by the Institute for Justice was the first national study of how occupational licensing affects the ability of aspiring entrepreneurs to enter into low and moderate return occupations such as barbering, and massage therapy (Carpenter et al. 2012). The study, which covered fifty states and the District of Columbia, found that licensing requirements are widespread and overly burdensome. For 102 occupations that were studied, fees averaged $209, a third of the licenses took more than a year to earn, and 79 occupations required at least one exam. Other findings were that "interior designer," licensed in only three states and the District of Columbia, was the most difficult occupation to enter; cosmetology trades, truck and bus drivers, and pest control applicators were the most widely licensed occupations; Louisiana licensed the most occupations (71) and Wyoming the least (24); and Arizona and California ranked as the most onerous states for acquiring licenses when taking into account the number of occupations licensed, as well as the burdens of license requirements. The arbitrariness of licensing was apparent since "most of the 102 occupations are practiced somewhere without government permission and apparently without widespread harm [and] only 15 are licensed in 40 states or more." Training and/or education requirements for "66 occupations have greater average licensure burdens than emergency medical technicians. The average cosmetologist spends 372 days in training; the average EMT only 33" (Carpenter et al. 2012).

Crony cosmetology capitalists have formed cartels in virtually every state in support of rules to boost enrollment and tuition revenue. In Texas, individuals cannot thread eyebrows without obtaining a state license. In order to legally perform this ancient Indian art, eyebrow threaders must spend 1,500 hours in a licensed cosmetology school and spend $20,000 for instruction that does not teach this skill. Hair braiding, regarded by many African Americans as a superior alternative to using hair straightening chemicals, is not taught in most cosmetology schools. This age-old process, which represents a venerable celebration of art and culture, involves "intricate twisting, weaving, extending or locking of natural hair" (Bayham 2005). The skill, which is passed on from generation to generation, can be a source of economic self-sufficiency for individuals who have limited financial resources and little formal education. This occupation is widely regulated, even though there have been no ill effects in eleven states that only require compliance with basic sanitation guidelines and general regulations applied to all small businesses. Hair braiders must earn cosmetology licenses in seven states; boards of cosmetology in twenty-two states are authorized to impose various amounts of cosmetology training for hair braiders; and specialized hair braiding licenses must be earned in ten states and the District of Columbia (Bayham 2005).

Prior to 2002, when occupational requirements for selling caskets were found to be unconstitutional (*Craigmiles v. Giles*), people selling this product in Tennessee had to first obtain a funeral license that entailed spending two years learning techniques of embalming and grief counseling. In early 2007, monks in Covington, Louisiana, were banned from selling wood caskets by a state board mostly composed of licensed funeral directors. The monks had been selling the caskets for around $2,000 each, which was a fraction of the price charged by funeral homes. State law at the time stipulated that caskets could only be sold by licensed funeral directors working for state-licensed funeral homes. To continue selling caskets, the monks would have needed to build a funeral parlor to accommodate at least thirty people, and provide a casket display room as well as other rooms, including one for embalming. They would have also needed to hire a full-time licensed funeral director to run the facility (Boehm 2013, 23). The monks challenged these requirements in court, and a panel of federal judges upheld a lower court ruling that favored the monks. Judges of the 5th U.S. Circuit Court of Appeals issued a statement that "funeral homes, not independent sellers, have been the problem for consumers with their bundling of products and markups of caskets" (23). Due to similar rulings in other states, caskets can be purchased in many places from low-cost competitors and are now even available online from Costco.

The many harsh occupational licensing laws supported by crony capitalists are harmful to both aspiring entrepreneurs and consumers. Many would-be entrepreneurs cannot afford the cost of licensing to start and operate their own businesses, and consumers are forced to pay higher prices because of reduced competition. Improving freedom for entrepreneurs seeking opportunity in various occupations is a slow process because the self-serving practices of crony capitalists are usually only given up when court actions are taken by individuals whose only goal is to earn an honest living.

Consider a final example of how crony capitalists attempted to use the coercive power of government to create benefits for themselves while damaging the public good. Before examining this case, consider a brief history of United States antitrust law. America's first antitrust law, the 1890 Sherman Act, was passed to prevent potential economic tyrants, known as monopolists, from mercilessly crushing their competitors and then charging ultra-high prices for their goods and services. Subsequent legislation, including the Clayton Antitrust Act and Federal Trade Commission Act of 1914, was designed to further strengthen the government's ability to reduce the social damage that these commercial leviathans could cause.

During its first major antitrust case in 1911, the Supreme Court applied a doctrine known as the "rule of reason." The Court ordered Standard Oil to be broken into competing companies, not because Standard Oil accounted for 90 percent of the market for refined oil, but because it was said to have achieved its dominant position using illegal business practices. Thus, the Court did not originally consider being big alone as tantamount to being a threat to the public good.

In 1945, the High Court abandoned the rule of reason when it concluded that the Aluminum Company of America (Alcoa) had violated antitrust laws even though it had been a good corporate citizen, adhering to the letter of the law and keeping prices low. This Court replaced the "rule of reason" doctrine with the per se rule, which meant that a company now only had to be big to be considered bad. It was no longer necessary to evaluate whether or not a company had used illegal business practices to achieve its dominant market position. This ruling was influenced by the mistaken idea, popular at the time, that a company could only be profitable and grow to a large size by taking advantage of its customers and employees.

In 1969, the Justice Department filed antitrust charges against IBM, a very big and therefore presumably bad company, in a case that continued for thirteen years and cost IBM more than $100 million. As this case progressed, there was a dramatic change in technology and several new competitors emerged in the market for computers. The Justice Department's decision to drop the IBM Case in 1982 signaled a movement from the "per se rule" back toward the "rule of reason."

A little more than a century after the first antitrust law was passed to protect consumers, private sector cronies collaborated with the Justice Department in an attempt to break up a major competitor. The Justice Department issued a civil action complaint in 1998 claiming that Microsoft, Inc., was in violation of the Sherman Act. Microsoft was accused of achieving its market position by using a variety of illegal business practices to suppress potential competitors. The Justice Department also charged that Microsoft's low software prices and free Internet browser was a ploy to exploit consumers. After eliminating the competition with this tactic, it was suggested that Microsoft would gouge its customers by charging high monopolist prices.

In June 2000, a US District Judge accused Microsoft of being "untrustworthy," and he ordered that it be broken into two companies. If carried out, this would have been the first time that government used antitrust law to disassemble a company that had grown entirely through internal expansion rather than by merger and acquisition. A year later, the US Circuit Court of Appeals rejected the presiding Judge's order to break up Microsoft, and it removed him from the case because of his bias against the company. In September 2001, the Justice Department conceded that it would no longer attempt to disassemble Microsoft, which was a tacit admission that the company had grown to a very large size in a highly competitive market by providing good products at reasonable prices made possible by economies of scale and efficient management.

In November 2001, the Department of Justice and Microsoft reached a tentative agreement to settle this case. Microsoft resumed most of its business practices after agreeing to share some of its intellectual property with other software venders, and to stop using several exclusionary tactics.

The Microsoft case was characterized by specious economic reasoning. The "charge a low price now but a high monopolist price later" rationale has always been a "straw man" unsupported by both theory and practice. Even if a firm achieves monopolist status, it must still be concerned about potential competitors that will be drawn into the market by high prices and profits. As long as the government does not restrict market entry, even companies the size of Microsoft must act as though they are operating as one company among many. As was seen in the IBM Case, any dominance a firm achieves can quickly evaporate because of rapid technological innovations that characterize many markets. This is seen today, as Microsoft's market position has been significantly eroded by multiple competitors.

At no time during the Microsoft Case was consideration given to the possibility that the company achieved significant gains in efficiency that enabled it to charge lower prices. This was a glaring omission since much innovation in software engineering has occurred not in spite of, but because of Microsoft's competitive tactics, and the primary beneficiaries of these technological advances have been consumers.

The antitrust case that targeted Bill Gates and his company can be compared to the ostracism of Aristides in fifth century BC Athens. According to Aristotle, after the Athenian leader Cleisthenes brought democracy to Athens, he introduced the political procedure of ostracism. Each year the Athenian Assembly decided by a show of hands whether or not to conduct an ostracism, which received its name from the Greek word for a piece of broken pottery (*ostraca*). If a majority voted yes, which was most likely to occur when the ruling political authority felt threatened by the leader of a competing faction, then a day in March was designated for a public vote. On the chosen day each male citizen had the opportunity to scratch on an *ostraca* the name of the man they most wanted to be sent away from the city. Since many Athenian citizens were illiterate, scribes would help with this task.

For an ostracism to be carried out, at least six thousand citizens had to vote, and the "winner" of this earthenware ballot was the person whose name appeared on the greatest number of potsherds. Ostracism's penalty was exile from Attica, the southeast region of the Greek mainland that made up the Athenian city-state. Departure had to take place within ten days of a vote and the absence was to last for ten years.

The idea underlying ostracism was that Athens needed protection from potential tyrants believed to pose significant threats to the fledgling democracy. In practice, ostracism enabled a political authority to protect its interests by sacrificing political rivals. One innocent victim of ostracism was Aristides, who was elected to Athens's college of exiles in 482 BC. Aristides was a renowned statesman who had first distinguished himself as a general at the battle of Marathon (490 BC). It was here that the Greeks and their allies defeated invading Persian forces, thereby saving Greece from Persian domination. The Athenians' nickname for Aristides was "the Just" because of his reputation for being fair-minded.

The primary offense of Aristides seemed to be his lofty presence in the midst of envious rivals. Plutarch wrote that on the day of balloting, an illiterate man handed Aristides a potsherd and asked him to scratch on it the name of Aristides. When asked if he had been injured by Aristides, the man replied, "None at all, [and] neither know I the man, but I am tired of hearing him everywhere called the Just" (Plutarch 105–125 AD/1992, 440). Three years after his ostracism, the Athenians repudiated this injustice and asked Aristides to lead a new fight against the Persians. He defeated them again in battle, and, by 477 BC, he persuaded rival Sparta to hand over to Athens its leadership of the Greek defensive alliance.

Following Aristides's ostracism, political opponents increasingly used this procedure to attack one another. The Greeks finally abandoned ostracism toward the end of the fifth century BC and replaced it with the practice of *graphe paranomon*. Under this alternative, individuals could only be indicted if they proposed decrees contrary to existing law.

It is instructive to consider parallels between the Microsoft antitrust case and the ostracism of Aristides. Bill Gates was extraordinarily successful in the marketplace just as Aristides excelled on the battlefield. The most successful businesses and entrepreneurs are those that usually attract governmental antitrust investigation and prosecution, just as ostracism was reserved for the most successful individuals who were not part of the ruling political apparatus. Powerful political rivals in Athens wanted to rid themselves of the real, or imagined, threat of Aristides, just as powerful business rivals wanted to diminish their major competitor that was founded by Gates. By using *political means*, these companies attempted to accomplish ends they were unable to achieve using *economic means*.

Several multimillionaire presidents heading multibillion-dollar companies worked closely with Justice Department officials for four years to create a 222-page report critical of Microsoft that the Justice Department used in the case. The ignoble deception used by the executives of competitor companies to justify this collaboration was that they wanted to "level the playing field" for the benefit of consumers. What they really wanted was to impose additional costs on Gates's company and to cut it down to a size that would give them a competitive advantage. If they had been successful, their use of *political means* would have created a bounty for themselves, while violating the property rights and diminishing the wealth of Microsoft's owners.

An unblemished Aristides returned to Attica just as a virtually unscathed Bill Gates and his company retained a lofty position in the marketplace. Neither Aristides nor Gates and his company were enemies of the people. Both were victims of legislation enabling rivals to pursue their own selfish interests at the expense of the public good. The history of ostracism demonstrates that even when original intentions of policy-makers are good, excessive power is eventually bent to serve the interests of individuals animated by less than noble impulses. Unconstrained power has a corrosive effect on all forms of political authority, including tyrants, popular majorities and democratically elected representatives.

Ludwig von Mises observed that "Competition . . . may sometimes or even often evoke in the competitors those passions of hatred and malice which usually accompany the intention of inflicting evil on other people" (1949/2007, 129). Antitrust laws should not be a weapon available for use by crony capitalists to diminish or destroy their more successful rivals.

There are many more examples of crony capitalists using ignoble deception and *political means* to boost their profits and insulate themselves from the rigors of competition. While preferential policies can be an expedient way to gain advantage in the marketplace, the cost to consumers, taxpayers, and nonpreferred firms and their employees is immense. Because public opinion rarely evolves "spontaneously among the multitude" because of the logical strength of an argument (Dicey 1919, 22–42), the Rule of Law is vulnerable to the force and volume of destructive legislation that receives its strength from the multitude of distortions and lies now being promulgated by politicians and their crony clients. Such ignoble deceptions pervert citizens' views about the appropriate role of public policy in social life, and erode the ideal of the extended order of peaceful social cooperation.

THE MISSING ENTREPRENEUR
OF ECONOMIC SCIENCE

Most textbooks used in college economics courses list four general types of resources that are referred to as factors of production, and the uses of three factors (land, labor, and capital) is said to be coordinated by the fourth factor, which is entrepreneurial ability. For example, land is usually defined as *nature's free gifts*, and includes things such as mineral deposits, oceans, rivers, and forests. While *free gifts* of "land" in an original state may meet the limited requirements of a small tribal unit, nature's raw materials can only satisfy varied wants in a modern extended social order when entrepreneurs apply intelligence and hard work to transform land and other resources into more useable and productive forms.

It is unfortunate that many economists, including those who praise private enterprise and competition, understate the importance of entrepreneurs in this transformational process. In one paragraph of a popular principles of economics textbook, entrepreneurs are defined as risk-takers, producers, and sellers of products and services. Following these brief comments, the contributions of entrepreneurs are not mentioned again throughout the entire eight-hundred-page text! A close look at this book reveals why the services of entrepreneurs are not needed in what could be described as an imaginary world of business fantasia. Economists ignore most of the major problems that entrepreneurs have to constantly deal with by assuming the availability of complete and perfect information concerning the highest quality and least expensive resources, the newest and most efficient techniques of production, and the tastes and preferences of consumers. In other words, all of the things that entrepreneurs must work hard to discover in a trial and error process are swept under the rug in business fantasia.

Almost anyone can be an astute decision-maker in this business fantasia. All that is needed is to graph or plug into requisite equations the information given by assumption. Production and consumption questions can then be answered by observing the position of intersecting curves or by calculating specific numbers that solve a system of simultaneous equations. Following this relatively simple procedure, the prices and quantities of goods that will maximize profit are magically revealed. All information derived using this approach is presupposed by the numbers originally assumed to be available.

The tangled jungle of business is much less orderly and far less predictable than the symmetrical orchards portrayed in economics textbooks. Information is scarce and sometimes terribly hard to get, and it is often only available in small bits and frequently contradictory pieces. Entrepreneurs seldom feel confident about having a clear view of the big picture. Because of incomplete and imperfect information, the best way entrepreneurs can measure the quality of their decisions is by checking their bottom line. Good product selection combined with prescient pricing and production decisions can result in revenue that exceeds the costs of operating a business, while not-so-good decisions are those that can lead to loss. Things are complicated by uncontrollable changes that cannot be foreseen; good decisions that produce profits today can result in losses tomorrow.

Profits and losses provide signals that entrepreneurs must pay attention to for long-term success. If an entrepreneur's production is technically efficient, but with increasing inventories and dwindling profits, then consumers are sending a message that prices may be too high or that competitors may be doing a better job serving their needs. This is a clear message that products or services need to be reevaluated and that it may be necessary to shift into other products or markets. Refusal or inability to make necessary changes along with repeated losses will eventually force individuals out of business.

High profits, on the other hand, signal that there is a divergence between what consumers strongly prefer and what is currently being supplied. Entrepreneurs are rewarded by profits if they are among the first to remove this divergence by shifting resources into products that consumers most value. Entrepreneurs who are slow to act will earn more modest returns. As Andrew Carnegie observed, "The first man gets the oyster, the second man gets the shell" (Carnegie 1950/1992, 302). Successful entrepreneurs have a knack for continually selecting products that can be sold at prices high enough to earn a profit.

It is relevant to consider why the struggles of entrepreneurs are ignored in most of the textbook representations of a competitive market economy. One reason is that it helps economists neatly analyze and comprehend a complex world rife with uncertainty and risk. While an understanding of market mechanics is improved through selective application of graphs and mathematical equations, using these techniques exclusively is as barren as a performance of *Hamlet* would be without the Prince of Denmark. This methodology, which is commonly used in both undergraduate and graduate courses, hides the real economic problem of an extended social order identified thusly by F. A. Hayek:

> The peculiar character of the problem of a rational economic order is determined precisely by the fact that the knowledge of the circumstances of which we must make use never exists in concentrated or integrated form. . . . The economic problem of society is thus not merely a problem of how to allocate "given" resources—if "given" is taken to mean given to a single mind which deliberately solves the problem set by these "data." It is rather a problem of how to secure the best use of resources known to any of the members of

society, for ends whose relative importance only these individuals know. Or, to put it briefly, it is a problem of the utilization of knowledge which is not given to anyone in its totality (Hayek 1945, 519).

The textbook methodology used in business fantasia obscures the push and pull of changing circumstances that entrepreneurs must respond to if their businesses are to remain viable. As an example, suppose a producer of cell phones and laptop computers experiences an unexpected boom in demand for her phones and a sharp decline in orders for her laptops. She suspects these changes may be more than temporary and so she quickly shifts much of her production from laptops to cell phones. Because some resources previously used in laptop production are not easily adapted to producing phones, her average cost of producing cell phones goes up. However, she can still earn more profit because she is able to raise the price of her cell phones. Her success attracts other cell phone manufacturers who invest money diverted from other less profitable projects. The increase in cell phone supply eventually reduces price and profit so that no additional resources will flow into the production of cell phones. The new quantity of cell phones is higher than before and is the "right" number, given consumer demand.

A similar process will characterize actions of others producing laptops who may leave the industry because of bankruptcy or because of more attractive (i.e., higher profit) opportunities. The quantity of laptops produced by manufacturers that remain in the industry will be lower than before and will represent the "right" number, given new consumer preferences.

Entrepreneurial adaptation to changing circumstances also guarantees that the most appropriate resources are used to meet the most strongly felt demands of consumers. Suppose this same producer of cell phones experiences a significant increase in the price of metal she has been using for her cell phone cases. To remain profitable, she must either use an alternative type of material or sharply increase the price of her cell phones. After modifying a portion of her production facility, she begins using the alternative material and is able to sell her cell phones at only a slightly higher price. Competitors who are slow to use the alternative material lose customers because they will need to sell their cell phones at a much higher price to cover higher production costs. Those who cannot adapt to changing resource prices will eventually go out of business.

While adjustments orchestrated by entrepreneurs are imperfect compared to textbook changes described by economists, the process that results from a pursuit of profit was viewed by Hayek as nothing short of a marvel.

> The marvel is that in a case like that of a scarcity of one raw material, without an order being issued, without more than perhaps a handful of people knowing the cause, tens of thousands of people whose identity could not be ascertained

by months of investigation, are made to use the material or its products more
sparingly; *i.e.,* they move in the right direction (Hayek 1945, 527).

THE INVISIBLE SOUL OF ECONOMIC SCIENCE

Economics, as it is currently taught, lacks a soul. In an essay published at the
beginning of this century, James M. Buchanan observed that while "Science
and self-interest, especially as combined, do indeed lend force to any argument," something more is needed to inspire individuals who have "an inner
yearning to become a participant" in an ideal social order (Buchanan 2000,
112–113). There must be a reverence for the *soul* or "moving spirit" of that
order (113). In a social order made possible by general rules of property and
just conduct, individuals who uses superior prudence in the *practice* of honorable entrepreneurship are the personification of its soul. Economists who
ignore the peaceful social order's moving spirit, make it vulnerable in a
competition with alternative systems, including socialism. The continuing
allure of socialism, despite clear evidence of the extended order's superiority
in terms of productivity and material abundance, may be due to socialism's
comprehensive vision that transcends both science and self-interest (113).
The soul of socialism and its "motivating spirits are categorically and dramatically different" from the extended social order's soul, but how can the
latter's ideal effectively inspire members of the body politic when its professional advocates, the economists, are reluctant to even acknowledge "the soul
of their position" (113)? Because competition in the pursuit of profit has
increasingly become a competition among coalitions seeking mutual exploitation, the magnificent but hidden soul of the extended social order is being
diminished as effectively as it has been decimated in other parts of the world
by "the rigidities of misguided efforts at collective command" (119).

Almost a half-century ago, economic journalist, Henry Hazlitt, observed
that there were thousands of fields of individuals engaged in multiple
schemes to improperly confiscate property and reduce liberty (Hazlitt 1997,
120). It's fair to say that there are now even more people involved in such
activities. Much of this stems from ignorance concerning the deleterious
effects of preferential legislation. More than ever before, people "advocate
tariffs, import quotas, subsidies and restrictions of competition . . . because
they are confused . . . [and] don't realize what the actual consequences will
be of the particular measures they propose, or perceive the cumulative debili-
tating effects of growing restrictions of human liberty" (127–28).

Many college graduates in business are blithely ignorant about the social
waste and damage of crony capitalism because their textbooks, even volumes
on business responsibility and ethics, do not touch on this subject. While it's
true that understanding virtues and honor in the *practice* of entrepreneurship
is not required to launch and run a successful business; such ignorance in-

creases the likelihood of participation in existing or newly formed crony alliances. Unenlightened victims of cronyism are more likely to share in the plunder than to try and stop it. Frederic Bastiat pointed out the danger to a nation when individuals engage in universal legal plunder:

> Instead of rooting out the injustices found in society, they make these injustices general. As soon as the plundered classes gain political power, they establish a system of reprisals against other classes. They do not abolish legal plunder. (This objective would demand more enlightenment than they possess.) Instead, they emulate their evil predecessors by participating in this legal plunder, even though it is against their own interests (Bastiat 1850b/1986, 12).

As legal plunder becomes widespread it "erases from everyone's conscience the distinction between justice and injustice" (12). To avoid this dilemma each person who reveres the extended social order must "master a great deal of detailed knowledge," and become "specialists in one or two lines" of activity (Hazlitt, 1997, 124). For entrepreneurs to recognize all forms of cronyism in their own industries and markets, they must acquire the intellectual virtue of knowledge. To avoid such business practices, and to resist the siren call of factions dedicated to legal plunder, they must display the moral virtue of courage. Thus, understanding the duties of an honorable entrepreneur is a necessary but not sufficient condition for being honorable. Honorable entrepreneurs must also act on this knowledge, and in doing so they are guardians of the extended order of peaceful social cooperation and its soul, which they make visible.

CRONY CAPITALISM, COURAGE, AND A SINGLE POLITICAL PRINCIPLE

Crony capitalism has a long history in the West, and Adam Smith's criticism of this practice in the eighteenth century applies with equal force today. During Smith's lifetime, a practice known as mercantilism was characterized by subsidies and tariffs that encouraged exports and discouraged imports for the purpose of increasing England's stock of bullion. While justification for these policies was a false theory that precious metals are the source of a nation's prosperity, the impetus came from politically influential entrepreneurs who demanded preferential treatment for their own benefit (Ekelund and Tollison 1981, 3–28). In Smith's words:

> It cannot be very difficult to determine who have been the contrivers of this whole mercantile system; not the consumers, whose interests have been entirely neglected; but the producers, whose interests have been so carefully attended to; and among this latter class our merchants and manufacturers have been by far the principal architects (1776/1981, 661).

While false claims today supporting preferential policies are different than eighteenth-century arguments, much of the impetus for such legislation still originates from producers who find it expedient to achieve their economic ends using the state's apparatus of compulsion and control. Preferential legislation continues to be portrayed as advancing the public good, and those who oppose schemes of confiscation are depicted as being antisocial, or selfish, or ignorant. The reputations of entrepreneurs and others who defend general rules of property can be tarnished, and pursuing justice in the courts or legislative arena can be expensive. Honorable entrepreneurs who incur the material and nonmaterial costs of defending the extended social order against the machinations of cronies and their political overlords are courageous and noble. As explained by Aristotle:

> The man, then, who faces and who fears the right things and from the right motive, in the right way and at the right time, and who feels confidence under the corresponding conditions, is brave . . . But courage is noble. Therefore the end also is noble; for each thing is defined by its end. Therefore it is for a noble end that the brave man endures and acts as courage directs (Aristotle c. 340 BC/1973, bk. III, ch. 7, 1115b).

Cicero observed that the most difficult ethical problem for a leader is to prevent a separation of the honorable and the useful. When useful but dishonorable actions are chosen that harm the extended social order, entrepreneurs fail Cicero's test of ethics, Tocqueville's test of honor, *and* Aristotle's test of courage. Principled entrepreneurs, who adhere to general rules that strengthen the extended social order and who oppose legislation that undermines this order, pass all three tests.

Consider a *single political principle* that can guide the honorable entrepreneur's decision to support or oppose a particular public policy: "An honorable entrepreneur does not support use of *political means* to advance his or her firm's interests if the ends pursued can only be achieved *in absence of this legislation* through the use of force, fraud or theft." Crony capitalists who violate this single principle contribute to a state of universal plunder where law, "instead of checking injustice, becomes the invincible weapon of injustice" (Bastiat 1850b/1986, 11).

SUMMARY AND CONCLUSIONS

Adam Smith had this to say about the virtue and honor of adhering to general rules of just conduct:

> The regard to those general rules of conduct is . . . a principle of the greatest consequence in human life, and the only principle by which the bulk of mankind are capable of directing their actions. . . . Without this sacred regard to

general rules, there is no man whose conduct can be much depended upon. It is this which constitutes the most essential difference between a man of principle and honor, and a worthless fellow. The one adheres on all occasions steadily and resolutely to his maxims, and preserves through the whole of his life one even tenor of conduct. The other acts variously and accidentally, as humour, inclination, or interest chance to be uppermost (1759/1982, 163).

Honorable entrepreneurs strive to achieve the external good of profit, while adhering to internal goods of just conduct and other virtues. In their use of *economic means*, they serve the long-run interests of an entire nation by producing sustained economic growth and creating a surplus that frequently benefits the poorest among us. The extended social order was made possible when individuals learned "to obey the same abstract rules" (Hayek 1988, 63), and this order is damaged by crony capitalists who use *political means* to achieve their ends. Crony capitalists, who use ignoble deception to justify their requests for special treatment, exploit consumers and taxpayers, and they betray principled competitors who hold themselves to a higher standard.

Economics textbooks that focus on maximizing profit through an impersonal application of quantitative techniques, diminish the importance of entrepreneurs as moral agents. Private virtues are moribund in societies where human action is mechanistic, whether in obedience to a political authority or as portrayed by systems of simultaneous equations. Entrepreneurs who are free to use their enlightened self-interest in open societies can experiment, discover their sometimes hidden talents, and learn to make choices that benefit themselves *and* the community at large. Honorable entrepreneurs strengthen the extended social order and make visible its soul. Profits that they earn provide for the future of their families, and by accumulating capital and enlarging their businesses, they are an engine of economic prosperity.

Achieving success honorably, through production and trade, is difficult and firms of entrepreneurs who are not up to this task soon perish. Notwithstanding these challenges, using *economic means* to achieve success is a private *and* a public virtue because it is a source of human flourishing and a cause of the wealth of nations.

Chapter Four

Justice, Honor, and Duty

Just as Aristotle first completed work on moral philosophy that he used as a foundation for his theory of politics, so did Adam Smith write *The Theory of Moral Sentiments* seventeen years before completing his economic treatise, *An Inquiry into the Nature and Causes of the Wealth of Nations*. Smith's later work is subtly informed by his *Theory of Moral Sentiments* that peaceful cooperation is most likely to occur in an extended social order when the pursuit of private interest is informed by superior prudence, which Tocqueville later referred to as enlightened self-interest. In *Moral Sentiments*, a book that is mostly unknown to contemporary mainstream economists, Smith discusses a wide variety of private and public virtues and he places a particular emphasis on the virtue of just conduct, which is "the main pillar that upholds the whole edifice" of an extended social order (1759/1982, 86). If each individual betters his own condition without violating general rules of justice, then liberty and social progress will be the natural result (1776/1981, 687).

Smith believed that rules of natural liberty were originally discovered through experience, inductive reasoning and "our natural sense of merit and propriety." After being sanctioned by religion and later confirmed by philosophical reasoning, these rules became "the ultimate foundations of what is just and unjust in human conduct" (1759/1982, 159–64). The virtue of just conduct took root in social life because of our ability to use reason and our willingness to follow principle guided by conscience, which is a part of us that Smith referred to as the "impartial spectator." The inmate inside continually evaluates our actions in relation to general rules of justice and enables us to counteract "the strongest impulses of self-love" and neutralize "the most presumptuous of our passions" (134–37). It is important to preserve our moral sense, for if it is lost "the great, the immense fabric of human society, that fabric which to raise and support seems in this world . . . to have been the peculiar and darling care of Nature, must in a moment crumble into atoms" (86).

DEVELOPMENT OF AN
IMPARTIAL SPECTATOR

Smith used the word *sympathy* to represent any fellow-feeling experienced by spectators observing the passions of others who are directly experiencing pleasure or pain (10). Spectators form this emotion by imagining how they would feel and act when encountering similar events. In Smith's words: "Every faculty in one man is the measure by which he judges of the like faculty in another. I judge of your sight by my sight, of your ear by my ear, of your reason by my reason, of your resentment by my resentment, of your love by my love" (19).

The experience of observing and evaluating the conduct of others prepares us to look inward and assess our own conduct from the perspective of an equitable judge, and we begin to appraise our own passions and responses to events in the same manner in which we approve or disapprove of the conduct of others. As examiner and judge of our own behavior, we are in a sense a different person than the part of us whose conduct is being judged. Smith wrote, "We can never survey our own sentiments and motives . . . unless we remove ourselves, as it were, from our own natural station . . . [and] we can do this in no other way than by endeavoring to view them with the eyes of other people, or as other people are likely to view them." As judge of our own conduct we imagine how we would be perceived by an unbiased observer, and we endorse our conduct only if we think the imagined judge would approve (110–13). While our lower self sometimes enjoys the "noisy applauses of ten thousand ignorant though enthusiastic admirers," the great judge inside prefers to earn the gratitude and admiration of a few distinguished observers by emulating the honorable individual who "adheres, on all occasions to his maxims" and who does not act "variously and accidentally, as humor, inclination, or interest chance to be uppermost" (159, 163, and 253).

We may or may not love our neighbor or mankind, but we definitely love "the grandeur, and dignity, and superiority of our own characters," which is acquired through adherence to general rules of natural liberty (137–38). Praiseworthy actions are more likely to result from this form of self-love than from the "soft power of humanity" or the "feeble spark of benevolence." While benevolence may be "the most graceful and agreeable of all the affections," it is only "the ornament which embellishes, not the foundation which supports the building" of human society (86, 137, and 301).

The impartial spectator's moral sense can be twisted by biased friends and relatives, intense passion, and civil and ecclesiastical factions (154–58 and 253). The inmate inside can also lose a sense of propriety if "brought up amidst violence, licentiousness, falsehood, and injustice" (200). If our moral sentiments are permanently corrupted, then faction and fanaticism are the most likely cause. It is virtually impossible for unbiased spectators to exist in the midst of the "violence and rage of contending parties," and "false notions of religion" cause a person to follow a wrong sense of duty (156 and 176).

CONFUSION AND GUILT OF AN
IMPARTIAL SPECTATOR

British economist, John Maynard Keynes, wrote: "ideas of economists and political philosophers, both when they are right and when they are wrong, are more powerful than is commonly understood. Indeed the world is ruled by little else." Most people are oblivious to Keynes's observation. It has been said that Americans have the philosophy of an army on the march, which is to say we are apt to sacrifice principle to achieve "practical" ends. This can be problematic because economic and political systems and their animating philosophies significantly affect the energy and prudence of a people. "Practical" ends that are at variance with general rules of property and justice can bewilder our moral sense and weaken the extended order of peaceful social cooperation.

Disparate ideas about the meaning of "social justice" and how it can serve "practical" ends causes impartial spectators to experience confusion and guilt. This, in turn, fosters an archipelago of fragmented thinking about public and private virtues and the role that government should play in social life. As applied to income and accumulated wealth, "social justice" carries with it suggestions for political action to alter a situation that has mostly emerged spontaneously in the extended social order. The impartial spectator is perplexed about how an unjust outcome can result from voluntary cooperation among people who have adhered to general rules of just conduct in their acquisition, use, and transfer of property. If honorable entrepreneurs achieve their individual ends without resorting to tactics of force, fraud, and theft, and if authorities proclaim that the outcome is unfair or unjust, then the concept of justice is stripped of any real meaning. "Social justice," in effect, becomes anything that the authorities want it to be. The danger of this was recognized early on by Confucius who wrote: "When words lose their meaning people will lose their liberty" (Hayek 1988, 106 and 109).

Regarding income, distributive justice can only have meaning if a political authority allocates funds to people in accordance with some desired pattern (e.g., "to each according to his _____"), and then later evaluates whether or not that particular patterned distribution is just. In an open society where individuals are free to pursue their own interests in accordance with general rules of property and justice, it is impossible for a controlling authority to "determine the relative incomes of the different people." Thus, incomes that emerge in the extended order of peaceful social cooperation are not just, but neither are they unjust (69).

Because economic freedom upsets patterns, attempts to establish and sustain a particular "just" income distribution requires continual interference in people's lives. Either activities believed to upset a preferred pattern must be forbidden, or income adjustments must be continually made using confiscatory tactics to correct perceived distribution imperfections that unconstrained activities have given rise to. To achieve a pattern of income that is unlikely to emerge in an extended social order, a political authority must exert significant control over individuals and groups. Creating and maintaining a precisely defined and strictly enforced pattern requires a totalitarian state.

CHALLENGES OF ACHIEVING "SOCIAL JUSTICE"

Attempts to achieve a "just" pattern of income distribution would require taking into account factors such as moral merit and need. To fairly implement such a distribution would call for administrators who are wise and good enough to make this determination. Someone would have to insure that the millionaires and the paupers are truly deserving of their status. But where can we find such a Zeus to judge our personal merits and give us our just rewards? It's unlikely that elected politicians, or a panel of Supreme Court justices, or a committee of the United Nations could be trusted for this task. At least one prominent legal scholar, Ronald Dworkin, has offered a solution. In *Law's Empire*, he simply assumes the existence of a judge who possesses "superhuman intellectual power and patience" (Dworkin 1986, 239). Dworkin's mythical judge, whom he names Hercules, is said to be capable of continually improving law using his powers of logic and his deep understanding of contemporary political theory. Dworkin suggests that Hercules can continually provide optimal solutions to social problems, because his high degree of enlightenment ensures that his private interests will always conform to the public interest. Attributes that enable Hercules to resolve controversial constitutional issues would surely qualify him to equitably distribute income.

While someone with perfect wisdom and perfect information, such as Dworkin's Hercules, might be a good candidate for formulating rules to distribute income equitably, man's reason, as pointed out by English jurist, William Blackstone, "is corrupt, and his understanding [is] full of ignorance and error" (Blackstone). The frailty, imperfection, and blindness of human reason make it a faulty instrument for distributing income. Philosopher Frie-drich Nietzsche warns that while experts "all pose as if they had discovered and reached their real opinions" through an objective intellectual process, most are just "wily spokesmen for their prejudices which they baptize [as] 'truths.'" Nietzsche cautions that influential and powerful philosophers can easily become the "baggage and lickspittles" of tyrannical social authorities (Nietzsche 1886/2000, 97). It seems reasonable to conclude that searching for a Zeus or a Hercules to wisely distribute income to worthy recipients would be as futile as Diogenes's search for an honest man.

A second possibility for determining a just income distribution would be to use popular vote. Problems with this are illuminated by theologian Rein-hold Niebuhr who suggests that even when people are moral in their private lives, they are often immoral in their collective decisions. Niebuhr writes: "As individuals, men believe that they ought to love and serve each other and establish justice between each other. As racial, economic and national groups they take for themselves, whatever their power can command" (1932/1960, 9).

Niebuhr provides an explanation for this incongruity. He suggests that the basis of moral virtue comes in part from our ability to apply reason to formu-late concepts of justice and to act in concert with these principles. The power of reason enables us to be aware of ourselves and our relation to other life. A sense of justice, which is "a product of the mind and not of the heart," can create social harmony "by placing inner restraints upon the desires of the self" and "by judging the claims and assertions of [other] individuals from the perspective of the intelligence of the total community" (30–31).

But our power of reason, which is needed to check our beastly impulses, is imperfect "and the proportion of reason to impulse becomes increasingly negative when we proceed from the life of individuals to that of social groups" (35). A common mind and purpose is always more inchoate and transitory within a group than it is for an individual. Niebuhr writes: "Only a romanticist of the purest water could maintain that a national group ever arrives at a 'common mind' or becomes conscious of a 'general will' without the use of either force or the threat of force" (6).

Although conscience is "a moral resource in human life" that can con-strain our antisocial impulses, it is most potent within an individual when it sets one impulse against another. It is much less effective in opposing the total force of an individual's desires. And as with reason, conscience is diminished within a group of individuals, and its presence contracts as the size of the group expands. To summarize Niebuhr's argument, social groups express themselves more selfishly than individuals because they have more power to impulsively defy general principles of justice, and they are less constrained by conscience and the power of reason. The larger the group, "the more inevitably will it be unified by momentary impulses and immediate and unreflective purposes" (48). German writer and politician Goethe viewed the largest of groups, the popular majority, with disdain: "There is nothing more odious than the majority; for it consists of a few powerful leaders, a certain number of accommodating scoundrels and subservient weaklings, and a mass of men who trudge after them without in the least knowing their own minds" (Babbitt 1924/1979, 290).

Given the difficulty of finding an individual who is honest and wise enough to distribute income fairly, and recognizing the likelihood that a popular majority will violate principles of justice, consider a third possibility. Suppose that a political authority in a centrally planned economy decides to give everyone the same compensation, and to discourage individuals from seeking more than their "fair" share. In applying this egalitarian version of the formula "from each according to his ability, to each according to his need," the planning authority would need to answer several difficult questions. First, would it be a violation of the fairness formula if someone is willing to work extra hard to have more than his or her designated share? Second, if people work beyond the number of assigned hours and jobs without permission, and if they receive an amount of income exceeding the authorized amount, should the excess be confiscated? Third, what can be done to counter the adverse effects that confiscatory policies and guaranteed incomes have on the willingness of people to work? Without a solution to this problem, everyone can be made equal, but everyone will be equally poor. As an aside, planners and party officials in the country best known for its central planning lived in luxurious townhouses and were driven to their Moscow offices in limousines. Apparently their needs exceeded that of common men and women, whose abilities were used to provide the Soviet bureaucrats with goods and services not available to the average Russian citizen.

Because a centrally planned economy is necessarily a command society there are many decisions that individuals are not free to make. The planners select occupations, as well as locations of work and home, and if an individual's plan conflicts with the central plan, then that person must defer to the central authority. Because there is no place for general rules of property and justice in such a society, there is no role for the honorable entrepreneur. Virtues are exercised and moral merit earned when individuals have freedom of choice and a responsibility to act rationally and wisely in an extended social order. As observed by F. A. Hayek: "It is the order in which we rank our different ends that our moral sense manifests itself; and in applying the general rules of morals to particular situations each individual is constantly called upon to interpret and apply the general principles and in doing so to create particular values" (Hayek 1996, 50). Obedience has no moral value when orders issued by the political authority are only followed because of threats of coercion. In the absence of liberty under the law, moral values wither.

There has never been a society in which income was determined by all-knowing agents of the state who intelligently applied principles of distributive justice. Humans have never been wise or honest enough, either individually or as part of a group, to carry out such a task. There have been societies, however, that have institutionalized envy, a passion considered unambiguously bad by Aristotle: "Jealousy is both reasonable and belongs to reasonable men, while envy is base and belongs to the base, for the one makes himself get good things by jealousy, while the other does not allow his neighbor to have them through envy" (Aristotle 4th Cen. BC/1984, sec. 6, ch. 2.11). Philosopher Robert Nozick explains the difference between envy and jealousy by presenting four alternatives:

Alternative 1—"Someone Else Has X and You Have X"
Alternative 2—"Someone Else Has X and You Don't Have X"
Alternative 3—"Someone Else Doesn't Have X and You Have X"
Alternative 4—"Someone Else Doesn't Have X and You Don't Have X"

You are jealous if you prefer alternative 1 to 2, while being indifferent between alternatives 3 and 4. You are envious if you prefer alternative 4 to 2, while preferring alternative 3 to 4 (Nozick 1974, 239).

Envy is a destructive passion that impedes social progress. Consider, for example, Anthropologist Margaret Mead's description of the primitive Dobu Islanders of the Western Pacific. Mead writes: "They create situations in which the objectively unlimited supply is redefined as being of fixed and limited quantity. No amount of labor can increase next year's yam crop, and no one can grow more yams than someone else without being accused of having magically stolen the extra yams from someone else's garden" (Mead 1937, 466). Because of envy, higher total production in this culture is only legitimate if all people share equally in its creation.

Helmut Schoeck observed that, in a study of the primitive New Zealand Māori tribe, anyone offending the tribal community in any way was subject to being plundered by his fellow tribesmen. The scope for which plunder was legitimate is breathtaking, and included virtually any deviation from the daily norm, including acts done intentionally, accidentally, by oneself, or by friends or relatives. It was common for individuals in this tribe to be plundered for the "offense" of being a friend of someone who died, or of having a child who was accidentally injured. No Māori tribesman held moveable property for very long and there was little incentive to work since labor only created a stock of things that provided an easy target for plunder. No one resisted being plundered because lost items could soon be replaced by carrying out attacks on others (Schoeck 1969/1987, 390). There are countries in the world today that have not advanced much beyond the primitive Dobu Islander and Māori tribes. They have inherited moral habits and traditions that are not conducive to economic development. Envy posing as social justice is incompatible with an extended social order.

When contemplating the many problems associated with income distribution schemes to achieve "social justice," the spontaneous results of an extended social order begin to look much better. Individuals who are free to use their own means in pursuit of their private ends can display unique combinations of abilities, skills, and knowledge that are mostly unknown and unappreciated. When honorable entrepreneurs are able to keep what people are willing to pay them for goods and services sold, they can quietly accumulate wealth to pass on to family members and to support wide-ranging scientific, artistic, religious, and charitable interests.

HIDDEN VIRTUE IN THE EXTENDED SOCIAL ORDER

When considering traditional ideas of *Virtue*, *Vice*, and *Negligence*, moral philosophers have generally considered intentions of individuals as being more important than actual consequences of their actions (Sowell 1987/2007, 20). *Virtue* applies to people trying to create benefits for others; *Vice* means that people are attempting to harm others; and *Negligence* refers to harm that is unintentionally inflicted on others. Prior to Adam Smith, most philosophers ignored benefits created unintentionally, because such thinking was not considered to be worthy of their attention (20). In *The Wealth of Nations* Smith took on this task by explaining how widespread social benefits can be created in the extended social order even when producers and traders are not particularly benevolent. Positive outcomes will occur as long as entrepreneurs pursuing their private interests act in concert with general rules of property and justice.

While success in the extended social order is not necessarily related to moral merit, evidence of widespread material self-centeredness in America's extended social order is lacking. Periods of significant wealth creation that are typically *followed* by abundant artistic and cultural creativity indicate that entrepreneurial activity is not focused exclusively on an unremitting pursuit of lucre. "Individuals, as well as communities, when they feel that other things have become more important than material advance, can turn to them" (Hayek 1996, 56). In an extended social order individuals frequently serve others to acquire material means for nonmaterial ends. It first appears that they are working primarily for themselves, but they eventually engage in acts of *Virtue* as traditionally understood. Their superior prudence is praiseworthy because they have freely chosen to sacrifice wealth previously earned. Billions of dollars are donated annually to worthy causes by private not-for-profit charitable foundations funded by successful entrepreneurs, and being poor in the United States is less harsh than being poor elsewhere. A 2012 study published by the World Bank points out that Americans who are in the second percentile of income earners (i.e., 98 percent of Americans earn more), are in the 62nd percentile when compared to people living in the rest of the world (Milanovic 2012).

HONOR, IGNORANCE, AND UNBRIDLED AMBITION IN POLITICS

Just as general human flourishing in the extended social order is nurtured by honorable entrepreneurs, so does the health of this order depend on honorable actions of political authorities. Honor in politics is particularly important because the state has a monopoly in the use of force, and legislation based on ignoble deception can significantly damage the public good. As observed by Baron de Montesquieu: "there are two sorts of corruption; one when the people do not observe the laws, the other when they are corrupted by the laws; an incurable evil, because it is in the very remedy itself" (Montesquieu 1748/1977, 160).

Political oratory can be a force for the good in social life when it strengthens citizens' adherence to a political society's ideals. Alternatively, base rhetoric, such as words that echo crony capitalist deceptions, gives legitimacy to the cronies' dishonorable quest for preferential advantage. The power and importance of oratory in the life of a political society was explored by Roman orator and statesman Marcus Tullius Cicero in a book, *On the Ideal Orator*. He finished this writing at the end of 55 BC, following a difficult period when his political enemies had confiscated his property and forced him into exile. In Book 1, which took the form of a Socratic dialogue, Cicero shared his thinking about what he considered to be the best education for an orator–statesmen.

Because everyone holding high government office had tremendous power, Cicero believed that it was incumbent on these individuals to understand and respect the Rule of Law, to safeguard private property, and to avoid encroaching on other fundamental rights of Roman citizens. Cicero's ideal of a principled and eloquent statesman, which he considered important for the health of the Roman Republic, resonates through the centuries and is relevant today for America's *Novus Ordo Seclorum*. Cicero's observations provide clarity about how education can equip honorable politicians to improve the public good while avoiding the seductions of crony capitalists.

Cicero's dialogue involves political leaders who were famous during his youth. A conversation is imagined to take place in 91 BC at the country estate of Lucius Licinius Crassus, who at that time was Rome's most distinguished orator. Participants in the dialogue are Crassus, who was a consul in 95 BC; Quintus Mucius Scaevola, an eminent jurist who had been consul in

117 BC; Marcus Antonius, one of the great orators of his time who was a consul in 99 BC; and two young men who represent Rome's future leaders (Cicero 55 BC/2001, 14–15). Cicero's opinion is expressed in this dialogue through the words of Crassus who debates Scaevola and Antonius in an attempt to convince the young men that they should follow his recommended path of enlightenment to prepare themselves adequately for political service to Rome.

Crassus begins the debate by commenting that much pleasure can be derived from becoming a professional orator because you can learn how to get people's attention and skillfully persuade or dissuade them in any way you choose. Crassus comments that "nothing is more admirable than being able, through speech, to have a hold on human minds, [and] to win over their inclinations." In addition, orators can use the power of speech to accomplish good in the law-courts, in public meetings and in the Forum. They can mobilize opinion to preserve individual rights and to defend Rome against those who would destroy it. A principled statesman, says Crassus, reaches the "highest achievements of human eloquence" when he uses his oratorical skills to move a people toward a more civilized society with its attendant laws, judicial safeguards and civic rights. Crassus summarizes "that the leadership and wisdom of the perfect orator provide the chief basis, not only for his own dignity, but also for the safety of countless individuals and of the State at large" (64–65).

Scaevola enters the debate by pointing out that many ancient communities were initially formed and developed under the tutelage of wise and courageous men who were not fluent speakers, and eloquent men had been known to diminish the greatness of Rome. Scaevola proposes that orators should avoid philosophical issues and schools of thought because it is too easy to become entangled in snares contrived by professional philosophers. He doesn't believe that an orator needs this type of knowledge because to be effective when pleading in court and "in public meetings and when declaring your opinion in the Senate" you only have to make your argument appear "stronger and more plausible." Scaevola contends that an orator who is ignorant about a particular subject can use polished presentations to "appear to intelligent listeners" that he is speaking skillfully, and "to ignorant ones truthfully as well" (66–68).

Antonius later joins the debate by commenting that while a general knowledge in many areas can be beneficial, a busy orator doesn't have the time to study other subjects (75). Antonius agrees with Scaevola that a speaker does not really need to know about a subject in order to effectively talk about it. An eloquent speaker, according to Antonius, can elevate and enhance any subject if he has a "sharp intellect, with a resourcefulness that comes from talent and experience, [and if he] can track down the thoughts, the feelings, the opinions, and the hopes of his fellow citizens and of those people whom he wants to persuade with his oratory" (112).

Antonius echoes Scaevola's contention that a knowledge of philosophy can be detrimental to the orator's success. Presenting a philosophical argument without exaggeration, for example, will likely leave an audience unmoved. And so the orator "by means of his words, greatly exaggerates and intensifies the bitterness of all those things that people, in the normal practice of everyday life, consider evil and distressing, . . . [and] in the same way he uses his speech to amplify and embellish what are commonly regarded as things to be pursued and desirable." Should an orator make the mistake of presenting himself as a philosophical "sage among fools," his listeners will either regard him as a tactless and pedantic Greek, or "they will admire his wisdom but resent being fools themselves." Even the great philosopher, Socrates, couldn't defend himself before Athenian judges because he was contemptuous of the type of speech required to sway them (112 and 115).

According to Antonius, an orator can even be an effective lawyer without a real knowledge of law as long as he presents convincing arguments in lawsuits and public debates by employing agreeable language that captures the sentiments of the audience he is speaking to. Antonius brags that if his knowledge of law had ever been deficient, he would have never felt inadequate when arguing a case because victorious advocates frequently win due to their eloquence rather than their legal expertise. If an orator ever needs help in formulating an argument, there are experts available to provide the legal javelins that can be hurled "with the strong arm of an orator." Antonius expresses admiration for Greek orators who argue cases knowing little or nothing about the law but who employ, if needed, skilled legal assistants. Antonius also comments that it is a waste of time for a political orator to study the history of law because "practices devised by our ancestors . . . either have lost their vigor precisely because of their old age, or have been invalidated because of new legislation" (118–20).

Crassus disagrees with Scaevola and Antonius, and he challenges their arguments. He says that the orator they praise is little more than an unskilled laborer, and their assertion that an orator doesn't need to know very much about a subject to make a polished presentation reflects mistaken Greek thinking about the power of oratory. Crassus points out that Greek philosophers once recommended banning ignorant but persuasive orators from having anything to do with branches of knowledge important for the health of a polity because of their danger to society. Socrates and Plato, two of the most authoritative and eloquent Greeks, were very critical of oratorical skills per se because they understood that an affinity for argument can easily overshadow the pursuit of truth.

For Crassus, "excellence in speaking cannot exist unless the speaker has grasped the subject he will speak about." If a political orator lacks knowledge in "public affairs of all sorts," and is ignorant about "statutes, traditions, and law," and doesn't understand "human character and behavior," then it will be impossible for him to speak in the courts, the Assembly, or the Senate in a "well-ordered, distinguished, and abundant fashion" (69). Although the words of an ignorant speaker can be beautiful and alluring, a flow of meaningless remarks that make no sense will make him sound like a fool. "For what can be more insane than the hollow sound of even the best and most distinguished words, if they are not based upon thought and knowledge" (70)?

Having challenged and diminished the arguments of Antonius and Scaevola, Crassus describes attributes of an ideal orator–statesman. As an orator this person must first have a considerable amount of natural ability. Only nature can implant "a certain quickness of the mind and intellect . . . which displays itself in the keenness of its thoughts in the richness with which it unfolds and elaborates them, and in the strength and retentiveness of its memory" (83). These natural attributes are enhanced and refined by reading poetry and history, and by perusing and scrutinizing the "teachers and writers of all the noble arts." Further benefits can be gained by studying these writings critically for merits and meanings, as well as for deficiencies and outright errors (93).

The orator–statesman should first and foremost "learn the civil law, acquire knowledge of the statutes, and get to know the whole of the past." In addition he "must acquire knowledge of the conventions of the Senate, the organization of the State, the legal standing of allies, treaties, pacts, and effective foreign policy" (83). Orators who don't take the time to gain this knowledge are shameless and lazy, and they pose a threat to "the preservation of equality of rights" (102). Knowing the law and how it affects the public is indispensable for a statesman because most people learn more from law than they learn from philosophy. Squabbling philosophers are apt to make grand and assertive claims in debates that seem endless, but it is from law that people "learn what is honorable is especially to be pursued, since virtue and hard work, performed with justice and rectitude, are adorned with high offices, rewards, and glory, while vices and offences are punished by fines, degradation, fetters, flogging, banishment, and death." The law also "teaches us to hold in check all our desires, and to protect our own property, while keeping our thoughts, our eyes, and our hands off what belongs to others" (104).

Crassus's final observation in Book 1 is an optimistic statement that an educated and principled orator–statesman can rouse the people to a sense of honor when they are "languishing or going astray." He can "lead the way from error or fire their rage against the wicked or soothe them when stirred up against the good" (107). But to become the "high priest of his art," an orator must be willing to work hard with a passion that is just short of love.

Most of America's Founders were eloquent and principled leaders who were virtually unanimous in their belief that the two primary reasons for government are the security of property and public safety (McDonald 1985, 3). In addition to being familiar with the writings of important philosophers, most holders of public office were generally familiar with Adam Smith's *Wealth of Nations* and some studied it in depth. Thomas Jefferson even considered it "the best book extant: on political economy" (Berns 1987, 333). Alexander Hamilton incorporated Smith's ideas in his public papers and James Madison was known to use phrases from the *Wealth of Nations* in his speeches (McDonald 1985, 128).

The Founders were also students of history, and they frequently bolstered their arguments by referring to lessons learned from the Greeks and the Romans, including Aristotle and Cicero. Their favorite book was Plutarch's *Lives of the Noble Grecians and Romans*, and when signing political tracts they often used symbolic pseudonyms representing historical figures. For example, Hamilton, Madison, and John Jay, authors of the *Federalist Papers* used the name Publius, who was revered in ancient Rome for establishing a foundation for the republic that followed the overthrow of Rome's last king. Founders without a scholarly bent were influenced and inspired by popular plays and orations such as William Shakespeare's *Julius Caesar* and Joseph Addison's *Cato* (67–70).

If orator–statesmen who were present at America's founding attained Cicero's "highest achievements of human eloquence," many politicians today more closely resemble the orators described by Scaevola and Antonius. They try to sound better and more plausible than their adversaries but they have only a cursory understanding of the issues, and when knowing little about a particular subject they use polished presentations to "appear to intelligent listeners" that they are speaking skillfully, and "to ignorant ones truthfully as well." Politicians today hire pollsters to identify "hot-button" issues, and they employ consultants to help them define, refine and rehearse positions for "canned" speeches and debates. A problem with this is that their ignorance of many subjects, including first principles of an extended social order, makes them vulnerable to ignoble deceptions, and they fail to see the danger of collaborating with colleagues who are less than honorable, and with cultural and business authorities bent on advancing their private interests at the expense of general rules of property and justice.

One can only imagine what Cicero would have to say if he could hear the inanities uttered by politicians today. His opinion of blithely ignorant political authorities in his own day, however, was quite clear. Through Crassus, Cicero declared:

> When a man has no knowledge . . . of the law of his own community—for him to roam all over the forum, moving haughtily and with head held high, with a

quick and willing tongue and a mien to match, looking now this way, now that, attended by a huge following, while holding out offers of protection to his clients, help to his friends, and the light of his intellect and counsel to virtually every citizen he meets—surely this must be considered more outrageous than anything (Cicero 55 BC/2001, 101)

While thought and knowledge of orator–statesmen can improve the health of a republic, reason and excessive ambition can be a source of frustration and antisocial behavior. Those who are overly ambitious, and who perceive their finiteness within "the immensities of the world," may damage the public good because of their need to universalize themselves in an attempt to give their lives significance beyond themselves (Niebuhr 1932/1960, 41). In politics, Abraham Lincoln touched on this point in a speech given to the Young Men's Lyceum of Springfield, Illinois, when he was twenty-nine years old. Lincoln warned that a nation is always vulnerable to the unbridled ambition that political authorities may have for personal distinction. If those in power cannot find opportunities for distinction in the task of peaceful construction, they will sometimes not hesitate to try to distinguish themselves by pulling down what their predecessors have erected. When achieving distinction is the paramount objective, it matters little whether it comes "at the expense of emancipating slaves or enslaving freemen" (Lincoln 1838).

Public choice economists study the politicians who are willing to do virtually anything to gain office and remain in power. In their theory of "political rent-seeking" these economists analyze the different ways that government can be used as an apparatus of discrimination and legal plunder. A politician who supports the preferential treatment of special interest groups, such as crony capitalists, expects to receive in return "votes, campaign workers, and perhaps most importantly, campaign contributions." Funding provided by special interests can then be used to "buy media time and take other steps to win the support of other voters" (Gwartney and Wagner 2004, 9–10). Unscrupulous politicians not only gain by helping cronies with preferential regulation, they sometimes extort funds from cronies they have previously helped by threatening to remove preferential advantages through deregulation. Open threats by politicians to reverse previous policies sometimes take the form of proposals that are never intended for passage. An example of this procedure, known a "milker bill," follows: "Representative Sam, in need of campaign contributions, has a bill introduced which excites some constituency to urge Sam to work hard for its defeat (easily achieved), pouring contributions into his campaign coffers and 'forever' endearing Sam to his constituency for his effectiveness" (McChesney 2004, 58).

Politicians can also extract funds from firms in an industry by threatening to support imposition of new costly regulations that will reduce industry profits. The proposed regulations will be withdrawn if firms pay what amounts to a ransom for political blackmail. The unbridled ambition of unscrupulous politicians illustrate Reinhold Niebuhr's observation that excessive and unchecked power "is a poison which blinds the eyes of moral insight and lames the will of moral purpose" (Niebuhr 1932/1960, 6).

DIFFUSING POWER IN AMERICA'S
TRIUNE SOCIAL ORDER

An important dimension of honorable entrepreneurship can be gleaned from Baron de Montesquieu who asserted that human flourishing is most likely to occur when there is a diffusion of power throughout society. This requires a moderate government with adequate checks and balances, and it also calls for nongovernmental bodies such as churches, universities, and private property owners to actively counterbalance political power. Montesquieu regarded social authorities who stand between government and the general population as a necessary reinforcement of a constitution's separation of powers. This was later echoed by James Madison in *Federalist 48* when he wrote that a written constitution is only a parchment barrier against tyranny. A despotic state does not have complex social gradations. If there are no noblemen, churchmen, intellectuals, or other social authorities to check and constrain governmental power, then a ruthless despot can flatten all others into one subservient class.

In America, Montesquieu's ideal has been described as a triune social order consisting of three systems—a competitive private enterprise economic system; a political system that is a constitutional democracy; and a moral-cultural system that embraces the ethic of pluralism. To function effectively, each system depends heavily on the other two (Novak 1982, 14–16). A competitive economic system requires well-defined and enforced property rights and a culture that doesn't view wealth creation as a zero-sum game; a constitutional democracy can only achieve political freedom if there is economic freedom in a culture that respects diversity; and the moral-cultural system's pursuit of truth through experience, divine revelation and philosophical reasoning is nourished by political liberty and economic opportunity. Despite this interdependence, the ends and the time cycles vary among the three systems and different paths must be traversed to reach each system's pinnacle. Because of these differences, the power accumulated by individuals and groups who ascend in one system is checked and constrained by centers of power in the other two systems. Political, economic, and cultural freedoms are threatened when power gathers over the three systems (31–70). Through the prism of Montesquieu, crony capitalism represents a dangerous confluence of power across America's economic and political systems.

Honorable entrepreneurs stand opposed to unprincipled business executives who commit legal plunder in violation of the honorable entrepreneur's *single political principle*. French economist Frederic Bastiat pointed out that it is fairly easy to spot legislation that is legalized plunder: "See if the law takes from some persons what belongs to them, and gives it to other persons to whom it does not belong. See if the law benefits one citizen at the expense of another by doing what the citizen himself cannot do without committing a crime" (Bastiat 1850b/1986, 17). Bastiat clearly saw the danger of unopposed and ever-expanding legal plunder: "It is not only an evil itself, but also it is a fertile source for further evils because it invites reprisals. If such a law—which may be an isolated case—is not abolished immediately, it will spread, multiply, and develop into a system" (17).

In some ways, legislation in America has already become "a veritable system" of legal plunder. It seems that the easiest way for politicians to be elected is to advocate preferential policies that benefit their constituents, including crony capitalists. While these policies may provide short-term benefits to their supporters, long-run costs extend beyond the burden placed on taxpayers, consumers and nonpreferred businesses and their employees. As pointed out by Bastiat: "When law and morality contradict each other, the citizen has the cruel alternative of either losing his moral sense or losing his respect for the law" (8).

The honorable entrepreneur serves as a makeweight against centers of power in the political and moral-cultural systems that threaten general rules of property and justice. As an example, in the early 1990s, proprietors of a plumbing supply business contested a decision by the city of Tigard, Oregon, to deny them a license to build an addition unless they agreed to forfeit 10 percent of their property for a bicycle path and water drainage. The owners, John and Florence Dolan, believed that such a requirement violated their Constitutional rights. The "Takings Clause" of the Fifth Amendment to the US Constitution stipulates that "private property [shall not] be taken for public use, without just compensation."

The city planning commission's decision was subsequently upheld by the Oregon State Court of Appeals and the Oregon Supreme Court. However, in 1994, the US Supreme Court ruled in favor of Florence Dolan (her husband had since died) with Chief Justice Rehnquist writing: "We can see no reason why the Takings Clause of the Fifth Amendment, as much a part of the Bill of Rights as the First Amendment or the Fourth Amendment, should be relegated to the status of a poor relation" *(Dolan v. City of Tigard)*. The Dolans' actions were honorable because they curbed the ability of cities and other governmental entities to use regulation to require property owners to make public improvements that are unrelated to business licensing requests. Public entities must now purchase land for such improvements.

HONOR AND DUTY IN THE EXTENDED SOCIAL ORDER

In 44 BC, a year before his assassination, Cicero wrote *On Duties* (*De Officiis*) for his twenty-one year old son who was studying oratory and philosophy in Athens. Cicero's intent was to give his son moral and political advice and instruction that he could not provide in person because of political considerations that limited his travel outside of Rome. Cicero also hoped that his writings would influence other young Romans more talented than his son who might someday govern Rome (Cicero 44 BC/1991, xvi–xviii). While Cicero was primarily interested in discussing duties of individuals in public life, his insights are also applicable to entrepreneurs pursuing their private interests honorably in an extended social order.

For Cicero, all forms of honor require a cultivation of certain duties, and neglecting these duties is dishonorable. Because human beings are able to "perceive consequences, to comprehend the causes of things . . . ; to compare similarities and to link and combine future with present events; and [to see] the whole course of life to prepare whatever is necessary for living it," we are obligated to determine our duties by answering five questions (bk. I.11–14, 6–8). First, we must identify which plans of action are honorable. Second, we need to determine actions that can help us achieve outcomes that are personally beneficial. Third, we must discern whether or not actions deemed to be beneficial are also honorable. Fourth, it's valuable to assess which actions are most honorable, and fifth, which are most beneficial. Uncertainty generally characterizes our consideration of all five questions, and ambivalence occupies the minds of those who perceive that beneficial actions may not also be honorable (bk. I.8–11, 4–6).

Cicero observed that honor is earned from actions associated with the virtues of wisdom, "the perception of truth" and ingenuity; justice, the preservation of "fellowship among men, with assigning to each his own, and with faithfulness to agreements one has made;" courage, "the greatness and strength of a lofty and unconquered spirit"; and moderation that requires "order and limit in everything that is said and done" (bk. I.15, 7). Cicero believed that justice is the most illustrious of these virtues because a just society fosters harmony and peaceful cooperation, which is a source of our greatest accomplishments. Thus, when choosing among duties the first priority should be "accorded to the class of duties grounded in human fellowship" (bk. I.160, 62).

There exists a natural bonding among people because of reason and speech, "which reconcile men to one another, through teaching, learning, communication, debating and making judgments" (bk. I.50, 21). These bonds are strengthened through exchange of "dutiful services, [and] by giving and receiving expertise and effort and means" (bk. I.22, 10). Bonds are further strengthened by "public affairs [that] must first of all see that everyone holds on to what is his, and that private men are never deprived of their goods by public acts." This is essential because humans, who may have first gathered in groups because of their nature, "sought protection in cities . . . in the hope of safeguarding their possessions" (bk. II.73, 92–93).

"The most widespread fellowship existing among men is that of all with all others" (1.51, 22), and when individuals violate the private rights of others they are "violating the law of human fellowship" (bk. I.21, 9). "[F]or one man to take something from another and to increase his own advantage at the cost of another's disadvantage is more contrary to nature than death, than poverty, than pain and than anything else that may happen to his body or external possessions" (bk. III.21, 108).

The most severe injustices are purposeful and cunning acts that require reflection and forethought. Such injustice occurs when someone intentionally harms another, or when there is failure to obstruct an injustice suffered by someone else when it is possible to do so. Violating general rules of just conduct is most typically associated with fear and avarice. There may be fear that by not committing an injustice we will be vulnerable to another's injustice, and unbridled greed can inspire a drive to acquire things using any means possible (bk. I.24–25, 10–11). As for individuals who ignore injustices suffered by others, their indifference may be caused by a desire to preserve their personal wealth, or by a self-centeredness that leaves no room for fellow-feeling. They claim to be minding their own business, and they "appear to do no one any injustice," but their injustice is that they "abandon the fellowship of life, because they contribute to it nothing of their devotion, nothing of their effort, nothing of their means" (bk. I.28–29, 12).

In his discussion of circumstances under which honorable and beneficial actions are aligned, Cicero suggested that at times it may appear that honorable actions are not also beneficial. But this is a mistake because "the rule of what is beneficial and of what is honorable is one and the same" (bk. III.74, 128). It is unfortunate when individuals ignore or fail to see the beneficial effects of honorable actions, because they will be prone "to pull apart things that are united by nature, [and this] error is the source of deceit, of misdeeds, and of all criminal activity" (bk. III.75.128). For Cicero, anyone "who defines the highest good in such a way that it has no connection with virtue, measuring it by his own advantages rather than by honorableness, cannot cultivate either friendship or justice or liberality" (bk. I.5, 3).

A CREDO FOR HONORABLE ENTREPRENEURS

Honorable entrepreneurs strengthen the extended order of peaceful social cooperation that makes possible our greatest achievements, and they must be ever alert to avoid ignoble actions that undermine this order. Duties that entrepreneurs must cultivate to support the extended social order can be gleaned from the writings of America's Founders, individuals who influenced them, and others who have embraced general rules of property and just conduct. The following maxims and duties can guide entrepreneurs and help them prevent a separation of the honorable and the useful.

Credo for Honorable Entrepreneurs

Preamble: In the pursuit of profit, I am keenly aware that my economic freedom has been affected for better or worse by actions of entrepreneurs who preceded me, and that the means I use to achieve material ends will shape boundaries of opportunity for future generations. As part of a spiritual community of past, present and future wealth creators who are dedicated to freedom and general prosperity, I embrace the following maxims and duties of an honorable entrepreneur:

- The keystone of the free society necessary for human flourishing is the Rule of Law; I conduct all of my activities and business practices lawfully and with integrity; I do not violate general rules of property and just conduct by engaging in actions that are advantageous to my firm but detrimental to the extended order of peaceful social cooperation; in pursuit of my enlightened self-interest I serve the long-run interests of the entire nation.
- *Economic means* and *political means* are available for my use to advance the interests of my firm; *economic means* are compatible with the Rule of Law and are generally characterized by mutually beneficial transactions among entrepreneurs, employees and customers; *political means* can subvert the Rule of Law and be a zero or negative-sum method that creates preferential benefits for the few at the expense of the many.
- I pride myself on using *economic means* to make available new and improved products, and to efficiently supply goods and services that people are willing and able to buy; in private life, I am guided by a constellation of material and nonmaterial interests; in business, my success is achieved by meeting the most strongly felt needs of my customers and by creating value for them in excess of prices they are asked to pay.
- I am most aligned against the selfish and deceitful practice of crony capitalism, which is a worm that is rotting the core of America's extended order of peaceful social cooperation; a *single principle* that guides all of

my political activities is that I will not use *political means* to advance my firm's interests if the ends pursued can only be achieved *in absence of this legislation* through the use of force, fraud or theft.

- I am committed to defending general rules of property and just conduct; I resist acquisitive business, political and cultural authorities when they use *political means* that undermine these rules and, when necessary, I am willing to endure their tactics of legislative and social intimidation; with courage, I stand between government and the general population as reinforcement of our Constitution's separation of powers.
- I am dedicated to pursuing my private interests honorably on all occasions, and I strive to inspire others to learn and practice the maxims and duties of an honorable entrepreneur; with knowledge of this Credo I encourage and give voice to fellow producers and traders who through habit and custom have a sense of its truth but whose half-intuitive wisdom makes them unsure and unable to express it in words.

THE POWER OF A NOBLE VISION

While enlightenment and honorable entrepreneurship go hand in hand, there remains the problem of convincing skeptical entrepreneurs to follow this path without assurance that their competitors will also take this "higher" road. They can be shown that giving up short-run preferential advantages is only a provisional sacrifice that will yield "a much greater ultimate benefit" (Mises 1927/1985, 33), but they may still choose a safer path and use *political means* in pursuit of their economic ends. Trying to convert these holdouts, while difficult, is worth the effort because they can become honorable entrepreneurship's most avid practitioners. As observed by David Hume, while individuals who join factions for selfish reasons "are apt . . . to neglect all the ties of honour and morality, in order to serve their party, . . . when a faction is formed upon a point of right or principle, there is no more determined sense of justice and equity" (Hume 1742/1987a, 33). This echoed Cicero's observation of how just and honorable people join together: "Nothing is more lovable and nothing more tightly binding than similarity in conduct that is good. For when men have similar pursuits and inclinations, it comes about that each one is as much delighted with the other as he is with himself" (Cicero 44 BC/1991, bk. I.56, 23).

While the Credo for Honorable Entrepreneurs is useful for inspiring a pursuit of enlightened self-interest, such codes of honor lose effectiveness in a democratic society because social positions and groups are jumbled together and continually fluctuate (Tocqueville 1840/1976, vol. 2, pt. III, ch. 18). This is especially true in the extended market order with its constant ebb and flow of individuals into and out of the entrepreneurial ranks whose opinions concerning acceptable business practices fluctuate and are sometimes self-contradictory.

Notwithstanding these challenges, a noble vision effectively expressed by an honorable leader can be a powerful force uniting people in pursuit of a shared purpose. This can be seen in how Joseph Addison's play *Cato* inspired George Washington, and how Washington used it to motivate his soldiers during the American Revolution. Addison's play was viewed by Washington many times over a forty-year period and he frequently used lines from it in his correspondence and speeches (Addison 1713/2004, viii). He had the play performed for his men at Valley Forge to inspire them to sacrifice everything for the cause of the Revolution, and later at Newburgh, New York, Washington replicated a scene from *Cato* before his revolting officers that brought them to tears and quieted their defiance (McDonald 1985, 193–96).

Cato the Younger, the subject of Addison's play, was an honorable man who was flawed in a number of ways. He was described by Plutarch as "rough and ungentle toward those that flattered him" and many people were annoyed by his inflexibility and unwillingness to compromise. Cato was also known to drink wine through the night and, added Cicero, "spend whole days in gambling" (Plutarch c. 105–125/1992, 270–99). Notwithstanding his shortcomings, Cato was greatly admired and respected by the men he commanded during his long and varied service to Rome. He gained a reputation for being highly principled and working harder than anyone else in the positions he occupied. Cato's greatest service to the Republic was his unyielding opposition to the intrigues and political ambition of Caesar and Pompey, and in a final act of defiance, Cato took his own life to deny Caesar the satisfaction of capturing and killing or extending clemency to the greatest remaining example of Roman republican virtue. During his final night on earth, Cato reinforced his courage to carry out this act by reading twice through Plato's dialogue *Phaedo* on the immortality of the soul (McDonald 1985, 314–15).

The principle of conduct illuminated by Addison demonstrates how ordinary people flawed in their private lives are still quite capable of advancing the public good. In 1713, a year after *Cato* was published, Addison touched on the importance of honor in an essay that appeared in the *Guardian*. He pointed out that while the actions of some individuals are primarily influenced by "conscience, duty, or religion," others are inspired to act by honor, and the "sense of honor is of so fine and delicate a nature, that it is only to be met with in minds which are naturally noble, or in such as have been cultivated by great examples, or a refined education" (Addison 1713/2004, 194). Adam Smith, who provided a philosophical expression of Addison's theatrical creation, later added that "the love of what is honorable and noble" on "many occasions prompts us to the practice of those divine virtues" (Smith 1759/1982, 137).

SUMMARY AND CONCLUSIONS

In the extended order of peaceful social cooperation, individuals who are honorable engage in voluntary exchange and advance their interests by furthering the interests of others, and a political authority supports this order by inhibiting antisocial acts of force, fraud, and theft. Cronyism represents an arrangement between firms that use dishonorable tactics, and politicians seeking electoral advantage by surreptitiously transferring wealth from taxpayers and consumers to well-organized special interests. Profit earned by these firms is not a residual that rewards innovation, production and trade, but is a politically guaranteed benefit earned by shamelessly violating general rules of property and just conduct.

Crony capitalism poses a serious threat to the extended social order because it represents a rot from within the ranks of entrepreneurs. If a political authority is the powerful lion of coercion, then the business executive who pursues preferential treatment is the treacherous little fox that masks his selfish intentions with rhetoric extolling the public benefits of his hoped-for private privileges. Cicero observed that while injustice can result from the lion's force or the fox's deceit, nothing deserves our disdain "more than that of men who, just at the time when they are most betraying trust, act in such a way that they might appear to be good men" (Cicero 55 BC/2001, 19).

America's Founders embraced general rules of property and justice as a means of diffusing power throughout society, and when they divided power among different branches and levels of government, they accomplished something political philosophers had never imagined. Until that time, it had been thought that the sovereign must be a single, all-powerful authority. The Founders treated sovereignty as a bundle of powers, and while they gave different branches and levels of government sovereign power in particular areas, no single authority was given complete power in all matters. Three years after ratification of the US Constitution, power in America's triune social order was further diffused with the addition of the Bill of Rights that insulated individuals in moral-cultural and economic systems from an overreaching political authority.

When crony capitalists trample the boundaries of America's triune social order, they empower a confiscatory state described by Bertrand de Jouvenel as a powerful and insatiable Minotaur (Jouvenel 1948/1993, 1–13). In Greek mythology, human children were sacrificed every nine years to be consumed by this fearsome monster that had the head and tail of a bull and the body of a man. Just as no human being can be great without virtue, no nation can be great without a respect for individual rights, and these rights are threatened when dishonorable entrepreneurs nourish the Minotaur for their own benefit. Avaricious social authorities in earlier societies used martial arts and bronze or iron weaponry to increase their wealth, while Machiavellian political, business, and cultural authorities today seek gain using legal plunder made possible by demagogic politicians.

Legislation can profoundly affect the public's view of the role that law should play in social life even when the legislation does not accomplish its intended or promised objectives (Dicey 1919, 22–42). Because political rhetoric can move us toward or away from a peaceful social order, it is important to unmask the base rhetorician who doesn't permit "an honest examination of alternatives . . . By discussing only one side of an issue, by mentioning cause without consequence or consequence without cause, acts without agents or agents without agency, he often successfully blocks definition and cause and effect reasoning" (Weaver 1953, 12). An ethical rhetorical argument is grounded in sound logic that is supported by clear thinking and experience, and it moves us toward the good (17–18). Logic and experience have revealed that "the life of the individual in society is possible only by virtue of social cooperation, and every individual would be most seriously harmed if the social organization of life and of production were to break down" (Mises 1927/1985, 33). In the extended order of peaceful social cooperation "everything that serves to preserve the social order" is good (34), and everything that damages this order is dishonorable and sometimes immoral.

America's constitutional democracy needed principled leaders to preserve the liberty patriots had won. While self-interest was expected to be their primary motive, they would possess enough public virtue to check the Founder's greatest fear, which was excessive state power unfettered by general rules of property and justice. Honorable entrepreneurs carry on this tradition, and by serving as a model for others to emulate, they are a powerful force that can stop America's backslide from the Rule of Law to the rule of man. A growing class of principled leaders, each of whom is guided by a clear-eyed impartial spectator, can rebalance power in America's triune social order, repair America's extended order of peaceful social cooperation, and foster widespread prosperity and general human flourishing.

Every honorable entrepreneur who uses *economic means*, and who shuns factions clamoring for preferential advantage using *political means*, is important because: "The unit to which all things must finally be referred is not the state or humanity or any other abstraction, but the man of character. Compared with this ultimate human reality, every other reality is only a shadow in the mist" (Babbitt 1924/1979, 335–36). When each of us prevents a separation of the honorable and the useful, we can be certain, at the very least, that there is one irrefutable benefit: "Make yourself an honest man, and then you may be sure there is one less rascal in the world" (Carlyle 1840/2006, 97).

Epilogue

Creating a Shared Vision of Honorable Entrepreneurship

Dear Diary: It took Joe several weeks to read the pamphlets provided by Alexis de Tocqueville, and we spent several months after that discussing how we might advance understanding and commitment to the *practice* of honorable entrepreneurship.

One of the things we talked about was transforming the pamphlets into a book that could be widely distributed to entrepreneurs and to students of business and economics. Joe thinks that such a pamphlet-sized book might inspire readers to want to support and preserve the great extended social order that has provided a fertile environment for America's freedom and economic prosperity. I told Joe that many students of business can now complete their degree program without ever hearing about cronyism and legal plunder. Joe nodded his head in agreement and said: "For students of business, the unfortunate implication of this omission is that any tactic using *political means* can be part of a profit-seeking firm's toolkit as long as it is legal, even when significant costs are imposed on taxpayers, consumers, and nonpreferred firms." I agreed and said: "Laws do not create morality."

Dear Diary: During one of our discussions, Joe and I brainstormed to identify individuals who have been honorable in business and politics, and who might serve as a role model for others to emulate. We agreed that honorable entrepreneurs are easy to find among privately held and family businesses. Joe commented: "I have conducted business with many of these praiseworthy individuals, and it's unfortunate that their personal influence usually does not extend beyond family, friends, and immediate business acquaintances." With

101

a look of dejection, Joe continued: "The contributions of many entrepreneurs who have strengthened America's social fabric are largely forgotten at the end of their productive lives when their companies are sold outright or absorbed by large public corporations."

Joe and I also talked about the difficulty of finding honorable entrepreneurs in large public corporations because of the incessant pressure that shareholders and Wall Street bankers and financiers place on company leaders to maximize quarterly profits. Joe immediately identified a notable exception: "A corporate executive who did what he thought was right, notwithstanding demands by those who were only concerned with profit, was John Allison, former chairman and CEO of Branch Banking & Trust, which most people know as BB&T."

I asked Joe to explain, and he replied: "Allison refused to be a party to one of the most egregious governmental assaults on private property in recent memory. In 2005, the Supreme Court sanctioned the authority of governmental bodies to take private property for 'public benefit' in addition to the traditional 'public use' criterion. Because of its ruling in *Kelo v. City of New London*, developers who fail to negotiate the purchase of private property can ask City Hall to confiscate it using the power of eminent domain because an increased tax base is considered to be a public benefit." Joe's face turned red as he continued: "In its *Kelo* ruling, the High Court committed what amounted to intellectual patricide because it destroyed an idea sacred to the Founders. In the eighteenth century, they gave private property rights unprecedented Constitutional protection in order to insulate individuals from an oppressive government. In 2005, the High Court created a blueprint for tyranny by taking these rights and handing them over to central urban planners."

I told Joe to calm down, and then asked him: "What role did John Allison play in all of this that made him stand out?" Joe answered: "Because of John Allison's leadership, BB&T refused to make loans to any contractor involved with property that had been forcefully acquired through a political authority's power of eminent domain. On top of that, the BB&T Charitable Foundation gave several million dollars to at least twenty-five colleges and universities to develop programs that teach students about the virtues and values of entrepreneurs who conduct business using *economic means* in the extended social order."

I agreed with Joe that the High Court's ruling in the *Kelo* case was egregious and that Allison was truly honorable in his response. Joe slowly shook his head and said: "Other bank executives who continued doing business as usual probably didn't even understand the fundamental principles of this case." When I commented that there now must be lots of examples of private firms that have relied on eminent domain to acquire property I was surprised by Joe's response: "It hasn't been as widespread as expected because of the national outcry condemning use of this procedure. It's also interesting that while it is sometimes difficult to find examples of honor in politics, within two years of the Court's decision politicians from forty-two states passed anti-Kelo legislation strengthening general rules of property by making it more difficult to use eminent domain for private use." Joe continued: "There is also a bit of poetic justice concerning the confiscation of Susette Kelo's property, because the development plan used to justify this action fell through and the City of New London ended up spending more than $78 million bulldozing property that now stands vacant. So much for the wisdom of central urban planners."

I asked Joe if he could think of any other examples of politicians acting honorably and he pointed out that this had occurred a little more than a decade prior to *Kelo* when political authorities began passing anti-regulatory takings legislation. Joe explained: "It all began when David Lucas went to court and courageously defended his property in South Carolina without assurance of success. In 1992, Lucas contested a new regulation imposed by the South Carolina Coastal Council that significantly limited use of ocean-front property that he had purchased for $1.6 million. The Council's position was that even though it had destroyed most of the property's value to benefit people living inland, it wasn't necessary to compensate Lucas. The Council argued that the Takings Clause of the Constitution's Fifth Amendment, which stipulates that "just compensation" be paid when property is taken for public use, didn't apply to Lucas because he retained title to the property. The case was ultimately heard by the US Supreme Court, which ruled that the Coastal Council had to acquire Lucas's property and provide compensation amounting to the property's value prior to the new regulation." I told Joe that I had heard about the case, and that years later the Coastal Council rescinded the regulation and sold the property for a profit. He briefly smiled and then said: "Lucas's actions were honorable not only because they established a legal precedent for recognition of regulatory takings, but also for encouraging political authorities in about half of the states to strengthen property rights by enacting anti-regulatory takings legislation requiring compensation when a new regulation causes economic harm."

Dear Diary: Following a number of conversations, Joe and I seemed to develop a mental block about what else we might do to inspire adherence to honorable entrepreneurship's maxims and duties other than publishing a book and making the "Credo for Honorable Entrepreneurs" widely available. We decided to take a break from our lengthy discussions so we could play a couple of chess games at the local club to clear our minds. Several moves into the game Joe's head briefly dipped and he suddenly sounded like the voice I remembered from several months back. I said: "Is it you Mr. Tocqueville? And if it is, why have you returned?"

It was indeed Tocqueville's voice and he said: "I have come back to give you and Joe an idea about how to improve the understanding and practice of honorable entrepreneurship. In volume 2 of my famous book I wrote about how forming an association dedicated to advancing an idea can spark creation of a shared vision and become a powerful force for the good." I asked Tocqueville where he got this idea and he answered: "When visiting your country in the nineteenth century, I observed that as soon as several Americans conceived a sentiment or an idea that they wanted to produce before the world, they began seeking each other out, and when found, they united. Thenceforth they were no longer isolated individuals, but a power conspicuous from the distance whose actions served as a positive example, and whose words were listened to."

I thanked Tocqueville for his advice, and I assured him that Joe and I would begin thinking about how to create such an association. Tocqueville responded: "I wish you well in this endeavor because what you are doing is essential for the future health of your country. The ever-expanding web now being spun by crony capitalists and their political allies threatens to create a system of complex and confiscatory rules that will confound the most intelligent and hold back the most energetic of entrepreneurs." When I told Tocqueville that this is now happening throughout America he said: "I know, and over time, while the will of entrepreneurs won't be shattered, it will be softened, bent, and guided. They won't be forced to act, but they will be constantly restrained from acting. A power such as this does not destroy, but it prevents existence; it does not tyrannize, but it compresses, enervates, extinguishes, and stupefies a people." Following these words Joe appeared to be exhausted. His head briefly dipped once again and Joe's own voice returned.

When I told him about Tocqueville's suggestion and warning, Joe became very excited and he said: "Forming an association of individuals dedicated to the practice of honorable entrepreneurship could accomplish one of the duties in the Credo, which is to 'encourage and give voice to fellow producers and traders who through habit and custom have a sense of its truth but whose half-intuitive wisdom makes them unsure and unable to express it in words.'"

Joe continued: "I can think of a perfect example of the importance of this duty, and it comes from a book that may be one of John Allison's favorites." I asked Joe to explain and he responded: "Allison made sure that all schools funded by BB&T's charitable foundation were provided copies of this book for use in their programs and courses. The book is Ayn Rand's *Atlas Shrugged*, and in it she describes an industrialist who has been demonized and demoralized by a sea of cultural and political critics despite having achieved success honorably." We agreed that this happens a lot today, and then Joe continued: "At a cocktail party the industrialist overhears an articulate advocate of honorable entrepreneurship praising individuals who live by trade and who are able to succeed because of their good judgment and superior ability. Most importantly, he hears supportive words that earning profit is only to be scorned if the 'source is corrupt.' In Rand's story the industrialist later confides that he was desperate to hear that accumulating wealth through production and trade can be virtuous." Joe then opened a copy of *Atlas Shrugged* and he read the maligned entrepreneur's words of thanks:

> It was more than gratitude, and I needed the gratitude; it was more than admiration, and I needed that, too; it was much more than any word I can find; it will take me days to think of all that it's given me—but one thing I do know; I needed it. I've never made an admission of this kind, because I've never cried for anyone's help (Rand 1954/2004, 387).

A teary-eyed Joe could barely continue to speak: "These beautiful and powerful words reveal the importance of forming an association dedicated to honorable entrepreneurship. It can be a support group that encourages and gives recognition to praiseworthy entrepreneurs who adhere to general rules of property and just conduct in their pursuit of profit. I put my hand on Joe's shoulder to comfort him and added: "Such a group can elevate and illuminate Addison's 'great examples' and reveal a nobility that inspires such acts."

Dear Diary: A few months later, Joe and I heard that a small college in Florida had just launched an honorable entrepreneurship minor program to teach college students how to start and run a business honorably. Joe became excited and he said: "This little college that is named for the nineteenth-century entrepreneur Henry Flagler, and is located in America's oldest European settlement, could become an important advocate of honorable entrepreneurship. Just as St. Augustine's lighthouse provided safe guidance for mariners, such a program could provide a bright beacon that illuminates a path toward renewed entrepreneurial flourishing in America."

I told Joe to get hold of himself, but when I suggested that his vision for this small school may be a bit too grand, he handed me a piece of paper from his back pocket with words written in 1907 by American architect, Daniel Burnham:

> Make no little plans; they have no magic to stir men's blood, and probably themselves will not be realized. Make big plans; aim high in hope and work, remembering that a noble, logical diagram once recorded will never die but long after we are gone will be a living thing, asserting itself with ever growing insistency (as cited in Moore 1921, 147).

Dear Diary: Joe passed away not long after sharing Burnham's words with me. For months I was profoundly saddened and lost focus about the importance of creating an association for honorable entrepreneurs. I started to feel better when I began thinking about the possibility that Joe may now be talking to Tocqueville on a regular basis and even playing chess with him. It makes me smile to think that Tocqueville is probably planning to spring the knight to rook four move on Joe, which he played months ago in that game with me. As I thought more about Joe's excitement, I concluded that he was right about making big plans that can profoundly affect American life, both materially and spiritually.

Dear Diary: A few months after Joe's death, his widow gave me framed words of an unknown nineteenth-century author that was hanging in Joe's office, and that I now display for all to see on the wall facing my office desk: "Sow a Thought, and you reap an Act; / Sow an Act, and you reap a Habit; / Sow a Habit, and you reap a Character; / Sow a Character, and you reap a Destiny" (Unknown Author, 19th Cen.). I am also inspired by Greek poet Sappho's words that I keep within reach: "Wealth without moral splendor / makes a dangerous neighbor; / but join the two together: / There is no higher fortune" (Sappho 7th Century BC/1995, 93). These words are a constant reminder of the importance of the task that Joe and I had imagined accomplishing, and they strengthen my belief that the fate of America may very well rest in the hands of entrepreneurs who make the right choice to pursue profit honorably.

Dear Diary: Now that I have regained focus, I am renewing efforts to launch an association dedicated to the *practice* of honorable entrepreneurship. I strongly believe that such an association is needed to explain why honor in business *and* politics is essential for preservation of the extended social order. It can demonstrate how principles of honorable entrepreneurship help business leaders avoid a separation of the honorable and the useful, and it can encourage adherence to the "Credo for Honorable Entrepreneurs." An association that brings together people in business, politics, and culture who share a noble vision that informs their pursuit of private interests can become, as Tocqueville described, "a power conspicuous from the distance whose actions serve as a positive example, and whose voice is listened to."

Dear Diary: After the experience of conversing with Alexis de Tocqueville, I am convinced that anything is possible, and that the great Cicero himself may somehow have been involved in all of this. It may just be a coincidence, but Joe's last name was Cicero and his Italian immigrant family descended from the Roman orator-statesman. In any case, who could have ever guessed that the idea of restoring America's great extended order of peaceful social cooperation was planted by a nineteenth-century Frenchman during a twenty-first-century game of chess? Tocqueville's warning at first worried me, but the more I think about it, the more optimistic I am about the future of America.

I have learned during the past few months that the root system of honorable entrepreneurship is enlightenment, and its taproot is conscience. For an American Renaissance to occur, it will be essential for individuals from all walks of life to acquire as much enlightenment as they can about the *practice* of honorable entrepreneurship, to embrace justice by engaging in acts of just conduct, and to light a candle to inspire others.

Joe once told me that Greek philosophers and poets used light as a metaphor for enlightenment, and darkness represented ignorance. Joe would say that even if a person's candle seems small, it should be lit because many candles burning together can illuminate the darkness. One of Joe's favorite quotes came from Scottish poet Robert Burns who wrote: "All the darkness in the world can't put out the light of one wee candle." And Joe would then add: "Darkness has no resistance to light. Darkness has no resistance to enlightenment."

Dear Diary: It's not yet clear to me how best to form an association dedicated to the *practice* of honorable entrepreneurship, but there is one thing I am sure of. The name of this association will be the "Cicero Society for Honorable Entrepreneurship." This will honor the memory of my dear friend who recognized the importance of forming such an association, and it will pay tribute to the great Roman orator-statesman whose writings permeate the idea of honorable entrepreneurship. I am quite certain that Joe and Marcus Tullius would both be pleased.

References

Addison, Joseph. 2004 [1713]. *Cato: A Tragedy, and Selected Essays.* Edited by Christine Dunn Henderson and Mark E. Yellin with a foreword by Forrest McDonald. Indianapolis: Liberty Fund, Inc.

Aristotle. 1984 [4th Cen. BC]. *The Art of Rhetoric.* Edited by Jonathan Barnes, translated by J. L. Ackrell. Princeton, NJ: Princeton University Press.

———. 1973 [c. 340 BC]. *Nicomachean Ethics* in *Introduction to Aristotle.* Second edition, revised and enlarged. Edited with a general introduction and introductions to the particular works by Richard McKeon. Chicago: University of Chicago Press.

———. 1988 [c. 325–323 BC]. *The Politics.* Edited by Stephen Everson. Translated by Benjamin Jowett. New York: Cambridge University Press.

Babbitt, Irving. 1979 [1924]. *Democracy and Leadership.* Foreword by Russell Kirk. Indianapolis: Liberty Fund Classics.

Bastiat, Frederic. 1964 [1850a]. *Economic Harmonies.* Edited by George B. de Huszar with an introduction by Dean Russell, translated from French by W. Hayden Boyers. Irvington-on-Hudson, NY: The Foundation for Economic Education.

———. 1986 [1850b]. *The Law.* Translated by Dean Russell. Irvington-on-Hudson, NY: The Foundation for Economic Education.

Bayham, Valerie. December 2005. "A Dream Deferred." Institute for Justice. http://www.ij.org/legal-barriers-to-african-hairbraiding-nationwide-2 (accessed: July 28, 2013).

Bennetts, Louise. April 26, 2013. "Too Big to Fail is Too Foolish to Continue." *Investor's Business Daily.* http://news.investors.com/print/ibd-editorials-on-the-right/042613653752-too-big-to-fail-is-just-another-subsidy-for-failure.aspx (accessed: August 6, 2013).

Berns, Walter. 1987. *Taking the Constitution Seriously.* New York: Simon & Schuster.

Blackstone, Sir William. 1765–1769. *Commentaries on the Laws of England.* http://www.allaboutphilosophy.org/natural-law-and-sir-william-blackstone-faq.htm (accessed: July 25, 2013).

Boehm, Eric. July/August 2013. "Grave Robbers: Anticompetitive Regulations for the Dead." *The Freeman.* Irvington-on-Hudson, NY: Foundation for Economic Education. pp. 23–24.

Buchanan, James M. Summer 2000. "The Soul of Classical Liberalism." *The Independent Review.* Oakland, CA: Independent Institute. pp. 111–19.

Burke, Edmund. February 1771. "A Letter to a Member of the National Assembly." Indianapolis: Liberty Fund Online Library of Liberty. http://lf-oll.s3.amazonaws.com/titles/660/Burke_0006_EBk_v6.0.pdf (accessed: December 30, 2015).

Carnegie, Andrew. 1992 [1950]. *The Forbes Scrapbook of Thoughts on the Business of Life.* Chicago: Triumph Books, Inc.

Carlyle, Thomas. 2006 [1840]. *On Heroes, Hero Worship, and Heroic in History.* Stockbridge, MA: Hard Press Editions.

Carpenter, Dick M., Lisa Knepper, Angela C. Ericksonm, and John K. Ross. May 2012. "License to Work: A National Study of Burdens for Occupational Licensing." Institute for Justice. http://www.ij.org/licensetowork (accessed: July 29, 2013).

Cicero, Marcus Tullius. 1991 [44 BC]. *On Duties.* Edited by M. T. Griffin and E. M. Atkins, translated by Margaret Atkins. Cambridge: Cambridge University Press.

———. 2001 [55 BC]. *On the Ideal Orator.* Translated with introduction, notes, appendices, glossary, and indices by James M. May and Jakob Wisse. New York: Oxford University Press.

Craigmiles v. Giles, 312 F.3d 220 (6th Cir. 2002).

Dicey, A. V. 1919. *Lectures on the Relation between Law and Public Opinion in England during the Nineteenth Century.* Second edition. London: McMillan & Co.

Dolan v. City of Tigard, 512 U.S. 374 (1975).

Driessen, Paul. 2012. "Why We Need to Terminate Big Wind Subsidies." http://www.cfact.org/2012/05/08/time-to-terminate-big-wind-subsidies (accessed: July 25, 2013).

Dworkin, Ronald. 1986. *Law's Empire.* Cambridge, MA: Belknap Press of Harvard University Press.

Ekelund, Jr., Robert B., and Robert D. Tollison. 1981. *Mercantilism as a Rent-Seeking Society.* College Station: Texas A&M University Press.

Ekelund, Jr., Robert B., Robert F. Hebert, Robert D. Tollison, Gary M. Anderson, and Audrey B. Davidson. 1996. *Sacred Trust: The Medieval Church as an Economic Firm.* New York: Oxford University Press.

Environmental Working Group (EWG) Farm Subsidies. "The United States Summary Information." http://farm.ewg.org/index.php (accessed: July 30, 2013).

Friedman, Milton. 1982 [1962]. *Capitalism and Freedom.* Chicago: University of Chicago Press.

Friedman, Milton, and Rose Friedman. 1980. *Free to Choose.* New York: Harcourt Brace Jovanovich.

Gibbon, Edward. 1776. *History of the Decline and Fall of the Roman Empire*, vol. 4. Kindle edition. New York: Everyman's Library.

Gilder, George. 1981. *Wealth and Poverty.* New York: Basic Books, Inc.

Gunderson, Gerald. 1989. *The Wealth Creators: An Entrepreneurial History of the United States.* New York: Truman Talley Books.

Gwartney, James, and Richard E. Wagner. 2014. "The Public Choice Revolution." In *Readings in Public Choice Economics.* Edited with a preface and notes by Jac C. Heckelman. Ann Arbor: University of Michigan Press.

Harris, Marvin. 1977. *Cannibals and Kings: The Origins of Cultures.* New York: Random House.

Hayek, F. A. 1960. *The Constitution of Liberty.* Chicago: University of Chicago Press.

———. 1988. *The Fatal Conceit: The Errors of Socialism.* Volume 1 of the collected works of F. A. Hayek. Edited by W. W. Bartley III. Chicago: University of Chicago Press.

———. 1996. "The Moral Element in Free Enterprise." *The Morality of Capitalism.* Second revised edition. Edited by Mark W. Hendrickson with a foreword by Hans Sennholz. Irvington-on-Hudson, NY: The Foundation for Economic Education.

———. 1945. "The Use of Knowledge in Society." *American Economic Review*, vol. XXXV, No. 4, pp. 519–30.

Hazlitt, Henry. 1993 [1971]. "False Remedies for Poverty." *The Wisdom of Henry Hazlitt.* Irvington-on-Hudson, NY: The Foundation for Economic Education.

———. 1997. *Is Politics Insoluble?* Edited with an introduction by Felix R. Livingston. Irvington-on-Hudson, NY: The Foundation for Economic Education.

Homer. 1990 [c. 8th Cen. BC]. *The Iliad.* Translated by Robert Fagles with introduction and notes by Bernard Knox. New York: Viking Penguin Books.

Hume, David. 1983 [1762]. *The History of England*, vol. 1. Reprint of 1778 edition. Indianapolis: Liberty Fund.

———. 1987a [1742]. "Of the First Principles of Government." Essay IV in *Essays: Moral, Political and Literary*. Revised Edition. Edited with a foreword, notes, and glossary by Eugene R. Miller. Indianapolis: Liberty Fund.

———. 1987b [1742]. "Of the Independency of Parliament." Essay VI in *Essays: Moral, Political and Literary*. Revised Edition. Edited with a foreword, notes, and glossary by Eugene R. Miller. Indianapolis: Liberty Fund.

———. 1978 [1740]. *A Treatise of Human Nature*. Second Edition. Analytical index by L. A. Selby-Bigge, revised text and notes by P. H. Nidditch. Oxford: Clarendon Press.

Johnson, Samuel. 2009 [1759]. *The History of Rasselas: Prince of Abissinia*. Edited with an introduction and notes by Thomas Keymer. Oxford: Oxford University Press.

Jouvenel, Bertrand de. 1993 [1948]. *On Power: The Natural History of Its Growth*. Indianapolis: Liberty Fund.

Kelo v. City of New London, 545 U.S. 469 (2005).

Kirk, Russell. August 1985. "The Courage to Affirm." *Imprimis*, vol. 14, no. 8. Hillsdale, MI: Hillsdale College.

Kirzner, Israel. 1979. *Perception, Opportunity, and Profit: Studies in the Theory of Entrepreneurship*. Chicago: University of Chicago Press.

Lincoln, Abraham. January 27, 1838. "The Perpetuation of Our Political Institutions." Address before the Young Men's Lyceum of Springfield, Illinois. http://www.abrahamlincolnonline.org/lincoln/speeches/lyceum.htm (accessed: July 25, 2013).

Locke, John. 1988 [1689]. *Two Treatises of Government*. Edited with an introduction and notes by Peter Laslett. Cambridge: Cambridge University Press, Cambridge Texts in the History of Political Thought.

Lomborg, Bjørn. ed. 2004. *Global Crises, Global Solutions*. Cambridge: Cambridge University Press.

MacIntyre, Alasdair. 2007 [1981]. *After Virtue*. Notre Dame, IN: University of Notre Dame Press. Third Edition.

Madison, James, Alexander Hamilton and John Jay. 1961 [1787–1788]. *The Federalist Numbers 10 and 51*. Edited and with an introduction by Clinton Rossiter. New York: NAL Penguin ed.

Madison, James. 1865 [1792]. *Letters and Other Writings of James Madison* vol. IV, pp. 478–80. Philadelphia: J. P. Lippincott & Co. https://archive.org/details/lettersotherwrit04madi (accessed: May 19, 2017).

McChesney, Fred S. 2004. "Rent Extraction and Rent Creation in the Economic Theory of Economic Regulation." *Readings in Public Choice Economics*. Edited with a preface and notes by Jac C. Heckelman. Ann Arbor: University of Michigan Press.

McDonald, Forrest. 1985. *Novus Ordo Seclorum: The Intellectual Origins of the Constitution*. Lawrence: University Press of Kansas.

Mead, Margaret, ed. 1937. *Cooperation and Competition among Primitive Peoples*. New York: McGraw Hill.

Milanovic, Branko. October 2012. "World Income Distribution." The World Bank Development Research, Poverty and Inequality. http://www.econ.worldbank.org/WBSITE/EXTERNAL/EXTDEC/EXTRESE (accessed: July 25, 2013).

Mill, John Stuart. 1989 [1859]. *" On Liberty" and Other Writings*. Edited by Stefan Collini. Cambridge: Cambridge University Press, Cambridge Texts in the History of Political Thought.

Mises, Ludwig von. 2007 [1949]. *Human Action: A Treatise on Economics*. Edited by Bettina Bien Greaves. Indianapolis: Liberty Fund.

———. 2011 [1940]. *Interventionism: An Economic Analysis*. Edited with a foreword by Bettina Bien Greaves. Indianapolis: Liberty Fund.

———. 1985 [1927]. *Liberalism in the Classical Tradition*. Translated by Ralph Raico with a preface to the third edition by Bettina Bien Greaves and a foreword by Louis M. Spadaro. San Francisco: Cobden Press.

———. 2008 [1952]. *Planning for Freedom: Let the Market System Work*. Edited and with a foreword by Bettina Bien Greaves. Indianapolis: Liberty Fund.

————. 1981 [1936]. *Socialism: An Economic and Sociological Analysis*. Translated by J. Kahane. Indianapolis: Liberty Fund.

Montesquieu, Charles-Louis de Secondat. 1977 [1748]. *The Spirit of Laws*. Reprint. Edited with an introduction by David Wallace Carrithers. Berkeley: University of California Press.

Moore, Charles. 1921. *Daniel H. Burnham, Architect, Planner of Cities*, vol 2. New York: Houghton Mifflin.

Niebuhr, Reinhold. 1960 [1932]. *Moral Man and Immoral Society*. Reprint. New York: Charles Scribner's Sons, The Scribner Library of Contemporary Classics.

Nietzsche, Friedrich. 2000 [1886]. *Beyond Good and Evil. Basic Writings of Nietzsche*. Translated and edited by Walter Arnold Kauffmann with an introduction by Peter Gay. New York: Modern Library edition.

Nock, Albert Jay. 1994 [1935]. *Our Enemy, The State*. With preface and introduction by Edmund A. Opitz. Delavan, WI: Hallberg Publishing Corporation.

Novak, Michael. 1982. *The Spirit of Democratic Capitalism*. New York: Simon & Schuster.

Nozick, Robert. 1974. *Anarchy, State, and Utopia*. New York: Basic Books.

Ovid. 1885 [8 AD]. *Mythology Greek and Roman*. Translated from the German of Friedrich Nösselt by Mrs. Angus W. Hall. London: Kerby & Endean.

Parks, Tim. 2005. *Medici Money: Banking, Metaphysics, and Art in Fifteenth-Century Florence*. London: Profile Books Ltd.

Plato. 1985 [c. 380–360 BC]. *The Republic*. Translated with a preface and introduction by Richard W. Sterling and William C. Scott. New York: W. W. Norton & Company, Inc.

————. 1892 [c. 387–380 BC]. *Menexenus*. In *The Dialogues of Plato*. Translated by B. Jowett with an introduction by Raphael Demos. New York: Random House.

Plutarch. 1992 [c. 105–125]. *Plutarch's Lives of the Noble Grecians and Romans: Volumes I and II*. Translated by John Dryden and edited by A. H. Clough. New York: Modern Library.

Pugel, Thomas A. 2012. *International Economics*. 15th Edition. New York: McGraw Hill Irwin.

Rand, Ayn. 2004 [1957]. *Atlas Shrugged*, 50th Anniversary Edition. Introduction by Leonard Peikoff. New York: SIGNET.

Read, Leonard E. December 1958. "I, Pencil: My Family Tree as Told to Leonard E. Read." *The Freeman*. Irvington-on-Hudson, NY: The Foundation for Economic Education.

Roberts, Russell. 2007. *The Choice: A Fable of Free Trade and Protectionism*. 3rd Edition. Upper Saddle River, NJ: Pearson Prentice Hall.

Sallust. 1921 [c. 41–40 BC]. *The War with Catiline*. Translated by J. C. Rolfe. Cambridge, MA: Harvard University Press, Loeb Classical Library.

Sappho. 1995 [7th Cen. BC]. *7 GREEKS*. Translated by Guy Davenport. New York: New Directions Publishing Corporation.

Schoeck, Helmut. 1987 [1969]. *Envy: A Theory of Social Behavior*. Translated by Martin Secker. Indianapolis: Liberty Fund.

Shakespeare, William. 1998 [1623]. *Julius Caesar*. Oxford School Shakespeare Series. Oxford: Oxford University Press.

Shapiro, Ilya. May 22, 2012. "Politicians and Team Owners Snooker Sports Fans and Taxpayers." *Huffington Post*. http://www.huffingtonpost.com/ilya-shapiro/sports-stadiums-taxes_ b_1537177.html (accessed: July 30, 2013).

Smith, Adam. 1981 [1776]. *An Inquiry into the Nature and Causes of the Wealth of Nations*. Reprint of Glasgow Edition. General Editors, R. H. Campbell and A. S. Skinner. Textual Editor, W. B. Todd. Indianapolis: Liberty Fund.

————. 1982 [1759]. *The Theory of Moral Sentiments*. Edited by D. D. Raphael and A. L. Macfie. Indianapolis: Liberty Fund.

Smith, Robert J. Fall 1981. "Resolving the Tragedy of the Commons by Creating Private Property Rights in Wildlife." *The Cato Journal* vol. 2, pp. 439–468.

Solzhenitsyn, Aleksandr I. 1985 [1973]. *The Gulag Archipelago: 1918–1956*. Translated by Thomas P. Whitney (pts. I–IV) and Harry Willetts (pts. V–VII) with an introduction and abridgment by Edward E. Ericson, Jr. New York: Harper & Row Publishers, Inc.

Soto, Hernando de. 2000. *The Mystery of Capital: Why Capitalism Triumphs in the West and Fails Everywhere Else*. New York: Basic Books.

————. 1990 [1989]. *The Other Path: The Invisible Revolution in the Third World*. Reprint. Translated by June Abbott with a foreword by Mario Vargas Llosa. New York: Harper & Row Publishers, Inc. First Perennial Library Edition.

Sowell, Thomas. 2007 [1987]. *A Conflict of Visions: Ideological Origins of Political Struggles*. New York: Basic Books.

————. 1980. *Knowledge and Decisions*. New York: Basic Books, Inc.

Starr, Chester G. 1971a. *The Ancient Greeks*. New York: Oxford University Press.

————. 1971b. *The Ancient Romans*. New York: Oxford University Press.

Stigler, George J. 1971. "The Theory of Economic Regulation." *The Bell Journal of Economics and Management*, vol. 2, iss. 1, pp. 3–21.

Thucydides. 1989 [431 BC]. *The Peloponnesian War*. The Complete Hobbes Translation with notes and a new introduction by David Grene. Chicago: University of Chicago Press.

Trotsky, Leon. 1937. *The Revolution Betrayed: What Is the Soviet Union and Where Is It Going?* Translated by Max Eastman. New York: Doubleday, Doran & Company.

Tocqueville, Alexis de. 1976 [1835 and 1840]. *Democracy in America*. Translated by George Lawrence and edited by J. P. Mayer. Garden City, NY: Anchor Books.

United States Department of Agriculture (USDA) Economic Research Service. "Farm Household Income." http://www.ers.usda.gov/topics/farm-economy/farm-household-well-being/farm-household-income.aspx (accessed: July 30, 2013).

Virgil. 1981 [19 BC]. *The Aeneid*. 35th Anniversary Edition. Translated with an introduction by Allen Mandelbaum, illustrated by Barry Moser. Berkeley: University of California Press.

Wall Street Journal. January 4, 2013. "Crony Capitalist Blowout." A-8.

————. December 12, 2016. "Guess Who's Defending Dodd-Frank." http://www.wsj.com/articles/guess-whos-defending-dodd-frank-1481590283 (accessed: January 9, 2017).

Weaver, Richard M. 1953. *The Ethics of Rhetoric*. Chicago: Henry Regnery Company.

Wexler, Alexandra. November 24, 2013. "USDA Unloads Forfeited Sugar." *Wall Street Journal*. http://www.wsj.com/articles/usda-unloads-forfeited-sugar-1385327188 (accessed July 14, 2015).

Wicksteed, Philip H. 1910. *The Common Sense of Political Economy*. London: Macmillan & Co., Liberty Fund Library of Economics and Liberty. http://www.econlib.org/library/Wicksteed/wkCS5.html (accessed: July 29, 2015).

Williams, John K. 1996. "The Armor of Saul." *The Morality of Capitalism*. Second revised edition. Edited by Mark W. Hendrickson with a foreword by Hans Sennholz. Irvington-on-Hudson, NY: The Foundation for Economic Education.

Index

About the Author

Felix R. Livingston is professor of economics and director of the Honorable Entrepreneurship Program at Flagler College in St. Augustine, Florida. This book grew out of his writings in *Independent Reflector*, a series of pamphlets that were first published in 2001. Joe Cicero, a character in the prologue and epilogue, was a friend and confidant whose influence is present throughout this book.